Success

Assessment Papers

KS3 English

LEVELS
5-6

Cherie S. Rowe

Sample page

paper number for quick reference

level showing attainment target

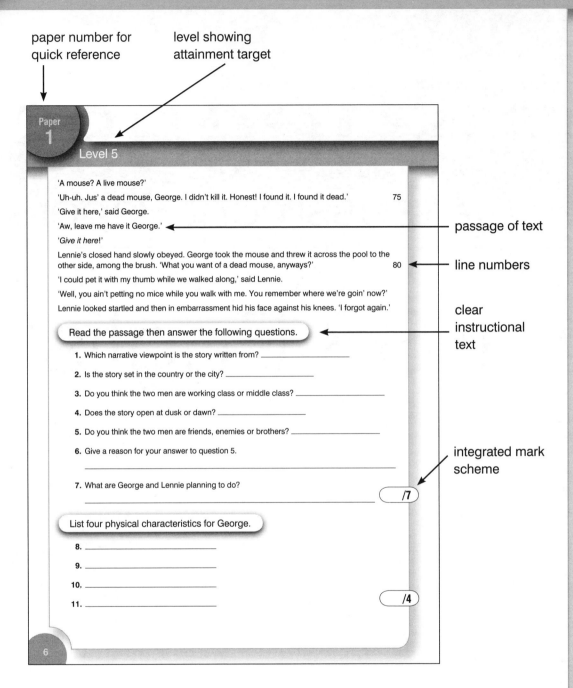

Paper 1

Level 5

'A mouse? A live mouse?'

'Uh-uh. Jus' a dead mouse, George. I didn't kill it. Honest! I found it. I found it dead.'   75

'Give it here,' said George.

'Aw, leave me have it George.' ◄———————————————————— passage of text

'*Give it here!*'

Lennie's closed hand slowly obeyed. George took the mouse and threw it across the pool to the other side, among the brush. 'What you want of a dead mouse, anyways?'   80 ◄——— line numbers

'I could pet it with my thumb while we walked along,' said Lennie.

'Well, you ain't petting no mice while you walk with me. You remember where we're goin' now?'

Lennie looked startled and then in embarrassment hid his face against his knees. 'I forgot again.'

Read the passage then answer the following questions. ◄——— clear instructional text

1. Which narrative viewpoint is the story written from? _____

2. Is the story set in the country or the city? _____

3. Do you think the two men are working class or middle class? _____

4. Does the story open at dusk or dawn? _____

5. Do you think the two men are friends, enemies or brothers? _____

6. Give a reason for your answer to question 5.

   _____

7. What are George and Lennie planning to do? ——— integrated mark scheme

   _____   /7

List four physical characteristics for George.

8. _____

9. _____

10. _____

11. _____   /4

6

Contents

PAPER 1

'Of Mice and Men' Chapter 1, by John Steinbeck

Evening of a hot day started the little wind to moving among the leaves. The shade climbed up
the hills toward the top. On the sand-banks the rabbits sat as quietly as little grey, sculptured
stones. And then from the direction of the state highway came the sound of footsteps on crisp
sycamore leaves. The rabbits hurried noiselessly for cover. A stilted heron laboured up into the
air and pounded down river. For a moment the place was lifeless, and then two men emerged   5
from the path and came into the opening by the green pool. They had walked in single file
down the path, and even in the open one stayed behind the other. Both were dressed in denim
trousers and in denim coats with brass buttons. Both wore black, shapeless hats and both
carried tight blanket rolls slung over their shoulders. The first man was small and quick, dark
of face, with restless eyes and sharp, strong features. Every part of him was defined: small,   10
strong hands, slender arms, a thin and bony nose. Behind him walked his opposite, a huge
man, shapeless of face, with large, pale eyes, with wide, sloping shoulders; and he walked
heavily, dragging his feet a little, the way a bear drags his paws. His arms did not swing at his
sides, but hung loosely and only moved because the heavy hands were pendula.

The first man stopped short in the clearing, and the follower nearly ran over him. He took   15
off his hat and wiped the sweat-band with his forefinger and snapped the moisture off. His
huge companion dropped his blankets and flung himself down and drank from the surface of
the pool; drank with long gulps, snorting into the water like a horse. The small man stepped
nervously beside him.

'Lennie!' he said sharply. 'Lennie, for God's sakes don't drink so much.' Lennie continued to   20
snort into the pool. The small man leaned over and shook him by the shoulder. 'Lennie. You
gonna be sick like you was last night.'

Lennie dipped his whole head under, hat and all, and then he sat up on the bank and his hat
dripped down on his blue coat and ran down his back. 'Tha's good,' he said. 'You drink some,
George. You take a good big drink.' He smiled happily.   25

George unslung his bundle and dropped it gently on the bank. 'I ain't sure it's good water,' he
said. 'Looks kinda scummy.'

Lennie dabbled his big paw in the water and wiggled his fingers so that water arose in little
splashes; rings widened across the pool to the other side and came back again … Lennie
watched them go. 'Look, George. Look what I done.'   30

George knelt beside the pool and drank from his hand with quick scoops. 'Tastes all right,'
he admitted. 'Don't really seem to be running, though. You never oughta drink water when it
ain't running, Lennie,' he said hopelessly. 'You'd drink out of a gutter if you was thirsty.' He
threw a scoop of water into his face and rubbed it about with his hand, under his chin and
around the back of his neck. Then he replaced his hat, pushed himself back from the river,   35
drew up his knees and embraced them. Lennie, who had been watching, imitated George
exactly. He pushed himself back, drew up his knees, embraced them, looked over to George

to see whether he had it just right. He pulled his hat down a little more over his eyes, the way George's hat was.

George stared morosely at the water. The rims of his eyes were red with sun glare. He said angrily: 'We could just as well of rode clear to the ranch if that busdriver knew what he was talking about. "Jes' a little stretch." God damn near four miles, that's what it was! Didn't wanta stop at the ranch gate, that's what. Too God damn lazy to pull up. Wonder he isn't too damn good to stop in Soledad at all. Kicks us out and says: "Jes' a little stretch down the road." I bet it was *more* than four miles. Damn hot day.' 45

Lennie looked timidly over to him. 'George?'

'Yeah, what ya want?'

'Where we goin', George?'

The little man jerked down the brim of his hat and scowled over at Lennie. 'So you forgot that awready, did you? I gotta tell you again, do I?...' 50

'I forgot,' Lennie said softly. 'I tried not to forget. Honest to God I did, George.'

'OK-OK. I'll tell ya again. I ain't got nothing to do. Might jus' as well spen' all my time tellin' you things and then you forget 'em, and I tell you again.'

'Tried and tried,' said Lennie, 'but it didn't do no good. I remember the rabbits, George.'

'The hell with the rabbits. That's all you ever can remember is them rabbits. OK! Now you 55 listen and this time you got to remember so we don't get in no trouble. You remember settin' in that gutter on Howard Street and watching' that blackboard?'

Lennie's face broke into a delighted smile. 'Why sure, George. I remember that … but … what'd we do then? I remember some girls come by and you says … you says …'

'The hell with what I says. You remember about us goin' into Murray and Ready's, and they 60 give us work cards and bus tickets?'

'Oh, sure, George. I remember that now.' His hands went quickly into his side coat pockets. He said gently, 'George … I ain't got mine. I musta lost it.' He looked down at the ground in despair.

'You never had none, … I got both of 'em here. Think I'd let you carry your own work card?' 65

Lennie grinned with relief. 'I … I thought I put it in my side pocket.' His hand went into the pocket again.

'What'd you take outa that pocket?'

'Ain't a think in my pocket,' Lennie said cleverly.

'I know there ain't. You got it in your hand. What you got in your hand – hidin' it?' 70

'I ain't got nothin', George. Honest.'

'Come on, give it here.'

Lennie held his closed hand away from George's direction. 'It's on'y a mouse, George.'

'A mouse? A live mouse?'

'Uh-uh. Jus' a dead mouse, George. I didn't kill it. Honest! I found it. I found it dead.'   75

'Give it here,' said George.

'Aw, leave me have it George.'

'*Give it here*!'

Lennie's closed hand slowly obeyed. George took the mouse and threw it across the pool to the
other side, among the brush. 'What you want of a dead mouse, anyways?'   80

'I could pet it with my thumb while we walked along,' said Lennie.

'Well, you ain't petting no mice while you walk with me. You remember where we're goin' now?'

Lennie looked startled and then in embarrassment hid his face against his knees. 'I forgot again.'

Read the passage then answer the following questions.

1. Which narrative viewpoint is the story written from? _____

2. Is the story set in the country or the city? _____

3. Do you think the two men are working class or middle class? _____

4. Does the story open at dusk or dawn? _____

5. Do you think the two men are friends, enemies or brothers? _____

6. Give a reason for your answer to question 5.

   _____

7. What are George and Lennie planning to do?

   _____   /7

List four physical characteristics for George.

8. _____

9. _____

10. _____

11. _____   /4

List four physical characteristics for Lennie.

12. _____

13. _____

14. _____

15. _____

/4

Choose a synonym from the box for each of the words underlined in the sentences below.

titanic	flicked	hugged	appeared	complied	uneasily
rapid	thumped	thrilled	glumly	brittle	timorously

road

16. And then from the direction of the state highway came the sound of footsteps on crisp sycamore leaves. _____

17. A stilted heron laboured up into the air and pounded down river. _____

18. … and then two men emerged from the path and came into the opening by the green pool. _____

19. His huge companion dropped his blankets… _____

20. The small man stepped nervously beside him. _____

21. George knelt beside the pool and drank from his hand with quick scoops. _____

22. George stared morosely at the water. _____

23. He took off his hat and wiped the sweat-band with his forefinger and snapped the moisture off. _____

his knees.

24. He pushed himself back, drew up his knees, embraced them … _____

25. Lennie looked timidly over to him. 'George?' _____

26. Lennie's face broke into a <u>delighted</u> smile. _____

27. Lennie's closed hand slowly <u>obeyed</u>. _____

/12

> Rewrite the following sentence replacing the contractions and formalising the language.

"OK-OK. I'll tell ya again. I ain't got nothing to do. Might jus' as well spen' all my time tellin' you things and then you forget 'em, and I tell you again."

28–37. _____

_____

/10

> Draw lines to match the main points from the story in the left-hand column to the quotations from the text in the right-hand column. Use the question numbers to write the correct sequence of events on the answer line below.

38. George acts protectively towards Lennie

39. Lennie tries to trick George

40. George curses the busdriver

41. Steinbeck opens the story with a description of dusk.

42. Lennie has trouble remembering things

'"Ain't a think in my pocket," Lennie said cleverly'

'Evening of a hot day …'

"So you forgot that awready did you?"

"for god's sakes don't drink so much … you gonna be sick."

"Too God damn lazy to pull up"

/6

43. Correct sequence of events: _____

> Explain how the quotations below support the statement that George is Lennie's best friend.

44. "You gonna be sick like you was last night."

_____

_____

45. "Look, George. Look what I done."

_____

_____

46. 'Lennie, who had been watching, imitated George exactly … looked over to George to see whether he had it just right. He pulled his hat down a little more over his eyes, the way George's hat was.'

_____

_____

47. "You never had none, … I got both of 'em here. Think I'd let you carry your own work card?"

_____

_____   /4

Explain how the quotations below support the statement that Lennie has a childlike innocence.

48. '"You never oughta drink water when it ain't running, Lennie," he said hopelessly. "You'd drink out of a gutter if you was thirsty."'

_____

_____

49. "I remember the rabbits, George."

_____

_____

50. "Uh-uh. Jus' a dead mouse, George. I didn't kill it. Honest! I found it. I found it dead."

_____

_____

51. '"I could pet it with my thumb while we walked along," said Lennie.'

_____

_____   /4

Remind yourself of the surrounding sentences from the passage and explain the effect of the short sentences below.

52. 'He smiled happily.'

_____

53. "Damn hot day."

_____

54. "Honest!"

_____

55. "I forgot again."

_____

/4

Explain the imagery underlined in the sentences below using one of the correct technical terms: simile, metaphor or repetition

56. 'The shade climbed up the hills toward the top.'

_____

_____

57. 'On the sand-banks the rabbits sat as quietly as little grey, sculptured stones.'

_____

_____

58. '… he walked heavily, dragging his feet a little, the way a bear drags his paws.'

_____

_____

59. '(He) … drank with long gulps, snorting into the water like a horse …'

_____

_____

60. 'Both were dressed in denim trousers and in denim coats with brass buttons. Both wore black, shapeless hats and both carried tight blanket rolls slung over their shoulders.'

_____

/5

Answer these questions.

61. Why do you think the story is set at the particular time of day?

_____

_____

62. What does the description of George suggest to us about his character?

_____

_____

63. What impression does Lennie's behaviour give about his character?

_____

_____

64. What impression does Steinbeck create about the setting at the opening of the story?

_____

_____

65. How does George feel about Lennie?

_____

_____

66. How does Lennie feel about George?

_____

_____

67. How does George feel about the bus driver?

_____

_____

68. Why is George worried that Lennie finds it difficult to remember things?

_____

_____

69. Why do you think Lennie insists that he did not kill the mouse?

_____

_____

/10

70. Do you think the ending of the story will be happy or sad? Explain your answer.

_____

/70

_____

PAPER 2

From The Times
March 24, 2010

Effects of passive smoking on the young costing NHS £23.3m a year

Sam Lister, Health Editor

More than 22,000 children seek medical help for asthma and wheezing as a result of passive smoking every year, according to the first UK assessment of the impact of second-hand smoke. The 200-page report on the health impacts of passive smoking on children, and the costs to the NHS, concludes that it is responsible for thousands of avoidable hospital and GP visits, as well as for one in five sudden infant deaths.   5

Doctors said that it provided the most compelling case yet for an extension of the smoking ban, which is due for review later this year, to enclosed public places, including cars, and open spaces frequented by children such as parks and playgrounds.

The report's authors added that stronger action was needed to prevent the promotion of smoking in films watched by the young, with "gratuitous smoking" requiring an 18 certificate.   10
The report, from the Royal College of Physicians (RCP), calculates that more than 20,000 chest infections, 120,000 bouts of middle ear disease and 200 cases of meningitis in the young are linked to the effects of second-hand smoke.

Passive smoking results in more than 300,000 GP consultations for children and about 9,500 hospital admissions. Of the £23.3 million spent by the NHS every year treating the   15
effects of passive smoking on the young, £9.7 million is due to doctors' visits and asthma treatments, £13.6 million is spent in hospital admissions and £4 million on asthma drugs for the under 16s.

Presenting the report yesterday, John Britton, the chairman of the RCP's tobacco advisory group, said that it should inform a series of strong policy decisions. He said that legislation to   20
ban smoking in the home would be unenforceable so, instead, views of what was acceptable had to be changed to protect the millions of children who live with smokers. Professor Britton added, however, that a total ban on smoking in cars and vans would be easier to enforce than the current situation where officers are expected to differentiate between business and private vehicles.   25

A Populus survey last year found that about three quarters of children whose parents smoked in their car wanted them to stop and were worried about the effect on their own health. Professor Britton said that even drivers who never had child passengers should get out of their cars before lighting up for reasons of road safety.

Richard Ashcroft, a professor of bioethics at Queen Mary, University of London, who contributed   30
to the report, said that the review also gave opportunities to clamp down on smoking in public places frequented by children such as play areas and outdoor swimming pools.

Professor Britton said that this could include banning parents from smoking around the school gates but added that it would be difficult to legislate for situations like family barbecues in private gardens. "Adults need to think about who's seeing them smoke," he said.   35

More than three quarters of 13,000 adults told a YouGov poll last year that they would support a ban on smoking in children's outdoor play areas.

Today's report, funded by Cancer Research UK and carried out by the UK Centre for Tobacco Control Studies, partly based at Nottingham University, found that children whose parents both smoked were almost nine times as likely to be exposed to second-hand smoke as those   40
in non-smoking families. If the father smoked then exposure was around three times higher. It was more than six times higher if the mother smoked. "Many parents believe that smoking in only one room or when the children have gone to bed will somehow protect the children from exposure," Professor Britton said. "It doesn't." He added that there was a misconception that opening a window would reduce risk.   45

The RCP called for increases in the real price of tobacco, measures to tackle tobacco smuggling and illegal trading and investment in media campaigns targeted at young people. Cigarettes should also be taken off display in shops, while packaging should be generic and standardised, doctors said.

Other measures in the report include cutting down exposure to images of people smoking in   50
the media — with films and television programmes that show gratuitous smoking classified as adult viewing — and stiff penalties for those who sell cigarettes to under-age children. Sir Liam Donaldson, the Chief Medical Officer, welcomed the report. "This is a serious public health concern," he said. The report's recommendations aligned well with the Government's 10-year vision for tobacco control set out in its strategy for England, A Smokefree Future.   55

"Among the many commitments in that report are plans to do more to reduce smoking in homes and cars in which children are present," Sir Liam added.

The report was "very valuable" and would be considered as part of the Department of Health's review of the legislation in England later this year.

The Department of Health said that children were being exposed to far less second-hand   60
smoke as a result of smokefree legislation. "The Government is looking at ways to go further to reduce the 9,500 children admitted to hospital every year as a direct result of exposure to second-hand tobacco smoke," said a spokesman.

"Parents have a responsibility to protect their children by stopping smoking around them in enclosed spaces like their cars and in their homes."   65

Simon Clark, director of the smokers' lobby group Forest, said that banning smoking in cars was "unacceptable and unenforceable".

"If you ban smoking in cars, which is a private space, it's a small step to banning smoking in the home," he said. "Smoking in outdoor areas poses little or no threat to anyone's health. Banning smoking in parks and other areas where children congregate would be a gross   70
overreaction. We wouldn't encourage people to smoke around children but adults should be allowed to use their common sense."

Read the article then answer the following questions.

Change these words into adjectives using the correct ending: **–ic** or **–ical**.

1. Biology   _____

2. Energy   _____

3. Athlete   _____

4. Fantasy   _____

5. Criticise   _____

6. Grammar   _____

7. Artist   _____

8. Majesty   _____

9. Topic   _____

10. System   _____

/10

Complete these sentences by filling in the gaps in the words, using the clue in brackets to help you.

11. The tob__ __ __ __ (cigarette) industry must take some responsibility for young people smoking.

12. Children are often enc__ __ __ __ ged (persuaded) to smoke because their parents do.

13. Smoking increases the risk of a co__ __n__ __ y (heart) attack.

14. Smoking is a__ __ ict__ __ __ (habit).

15. The public have a right to breath unpo__ __ __ t__ d (clean) air.

16. Exp__ __ __an__ (pregnant) women who smoke cause damage to their unborn children.

17. The ap__ __ __ __ __ __ __ e (arrival) of smoking advertisements in the 1950s on television increased the popularity of smoking.

18. There is a wide variety of med__ __ __ __ __l (healing) remedies to support smokers who want to give up.

19. If smokers increased their __n__ __l__ dge (understanding) about the dangers of smoking, more would stop.

20. Par__ic__p__t__ __ n (taking part) in self-help groups to stop smoking has increased.

/10

Match the words in bold in the box below to their synonyms from the article.

useful	contact	forbid	misunderstanding
broad	effect	major	persuasive
unnecessary	gather	liability	promise

21. impact   _____

22. compelling   _____

23. gross   _____

24. gratuitous   _____

25. exposure   _____

26. generic   _____

27. congregate   _____

28. commitment   _____

29. responsibility   _____

30. ban   _____

31. valuable   _____

32. misconception   _____

/12

Draw lines to match each paragraph description in the left-hand column to its position in the text in the right-hand column.

33. Summarises the entire topic   First paragraph

34. Most important point   Links paragraphs

35. Outlines the entire topic   Connectives such as however / although / whereas

36. Repeats a word / phrase / idea   Last paragraph
    from a previous paragraph

37. Examples   Comes first in the paragraph

38. Alternative viewpoint   Come after giving an opinion

/6

Write a sentence **summarising** the content of the lines from the article.

39. Summary of lines 1–5:

_____

_____

40. Summary of lines 19–25:

_____

_____

41. Summary of lines 38–45:

_____

_____

42. Summary of lines 50–55:

_____

_____

/4

Rewrite the following complex sentence into four short, direct sentences to make the message stronger.

The 200-page report on the health impacts of passive smoking on children, and the costs to the NHS, concludes that it is responsible for thousands of avoidable hospital and GP visits, as well as for one in five sudden infant deaths.

43. Sentence 1: _____

44. Sentence 2: _____

45. Sentence 3: _____

46. Sentence 4: _____

/4

Answer these questions.

47. Does the headline suggest support or opposition to an extension of the smoking ban?

_____

48. Explain your answer to question 47. _____

_____

/2

State whether the following groups of people support or oppose the extension of the smoking ban.

49. The NHS   _____

50. Simon Clark   _____

51. Professor John Britton   _____

52. Professor Richard Ashcroft   _____

53. More than 9750 adults   _____

54. Cancer Research UK   _____

55. Over 9750 adults who answered a poll   _____

56. Sir Liam Donaldson _____

57. Royal College of Physicians _____

58. Department of Health _____

59. Doctors _____

60. 75% of children interviewed by Populus _____

/12

Complete the paragraph below using the words from the box to fill in the gaps.

cost	persuade	reduce	emotive	young
continues	emphasise	strong	statistics	headline

61–70. The article presents a _____ case for the extension of a smoking

ban. Immediately, the _____ draws our attention to the effects

on the _____ and the _____ of passive

smoking. The first sentence of the article uses powerful _____ to

_____ us that something should be done to _____

the effects of passive smoking. The journalist _____ to use statistics

throughout the article to _____ the effects of passive smoking.

The opening paragraph concludes with an _____ statistic: passive

smoking is responsible for one in five sudden infant deaths.

/10

/70

TOP of the PRESS

Saturday 9.01.10
60p

That's Not *MWAH*gic!

Kissing sickness hits the States! Fifty children in America ended up in hospital complaining of sickness and stomach cramps after secretly kissing a frog. The children said they thought their frog pucker would be magical but instead of catching a prince, they caught salmonella. "I only wanted a prince!" Tiffany, aged 11, cried. "I'm really surprised, I didn't realise that Jack would copy the films." Jack's father claimed. "I thought I would turn into a prince." Jack, age 12, told the doctors.

The Healthy Children Foundation claimed that cases of salmonella poisoning from frogs could reach phenomenal numbers. "Parents should call their doctor if their child is experiencing sickness, headaches or diarrhoea. With the correct treatment, usually

Don't trust this cheeky froggie!

antibiotics, they can fight the disease. *It would obviously help if children didn't kiss reptiles in the first place.*"

The Freedom For Frogs organisation is worried about the reputation of frogs. "It's not their fault. Frogs are going about their own business, doing their own thing. There's no reason to hate frogs, just don't kiss them."

Top of the Press have started a petition to demand that Jelly Jolly Films add an information warning to their popular film, "The Frog Prince" before it is released in Britain. Join our campaign and send an email to nokissingfrogs@topofthepress.co.uk

Read the article then answer the following questions.

Identify the key points from each paragraph.

1. _____

2. _____

3. _____

4. _____

5. What type of newspaper do you think the article comes from?

_____

/5

Do the following newspaper features typically belong to a **tabloid** or **broadsheet** newspaper?

6. Uses lots of facts rather than lots of emotions _____

7. Content is more subjective _____

8. Uses more complex sentences than simple sentences _____

9. Uses a mixture of fact and emotion _____

10. Has more to do with major world and national events _____

11. Often uses slang _____

12. Uses lots of emotive language _____

13. Content of articles are often heavily biased _____

14. Uses lots of exaggeration _____

/10

15. Often uses difficult vocabulary _____

Find an example from the passage for each of the following features.

16. Exaggerated language _____

17. Use of slang _____

18. Use of emotive language _____

19. Use of humour _____

20. Alliteration _____

21. Expert opinion _____

/6

Answer these questions.

22. How many children have been diagnosed with salmonella? _____

23. Why does the article include a quotation from Tiffany?

_____

_____

24. Why does the article include a quotation from Jack and his father?

_____

_____

25. Do you think this is a serious or humorous article? _____

26. Explain your answer to question 25.

_____

_____

27. Do you think the Healthy Children Foundation is sympathetic? _____

28. Explain your answer to question 27.

_____

_____

29. Why does the newspaper include the quotation from Freedom For Frogs?

_____

_____

30. Do you think their concerns are serious? _____

31. Explain your answer to question 30.

_____

_____

32–34. What are the danger symptoms for salmonella?

_____

35. Why has the paper started a petition?

_____

_____

36. How would you show support for the petition?

_____

37. Why is line 13–14 in italics?

_____

_____

38–39. Explain the effect of the picture in the article.

_____

_____

40. How does the headline capture the reader's attention?

_____

_____

41. Explain how the first sentence makes you want to read on.

_____

_____

/20

Label the following statements as facts or opinions.

42. Fifty children in America caught salmonella. _____

43. The children kissed frogs because they watched the film, 'The Frog Prince.'

_____

44. The children were not very clever. _____

45. Tiffany kissed the frog because she wanted a prince. _____

46. Jack kissed the frog because he wanted to be a prince. _____

47. All children in America love kissing frogs. _____

48. All children in Britain will catch salmonella. _____

49. Doctors can treat salmonella with antibiotics. _____

50. Salmonella causes diarrhoea, sickness and vomiting. _____

51. Jelly Jolly Films should warn children not to kiss frogs. _____

/10

Unscramble these letters to make a feature you would find in a newspaper.

52. Subplot inlet _____

53. Pain cot _____

54. Ideal hen _____

55. Error pet _____

56. Alert spin _____

/5

Write these sentences again with the correct punctuation added.

57. Tiffany said she kissed the frog because she wanted a prince

_____

_____

58–60. I didnt want to get sick I only wanted a prince

_____

61. Jacks friends thought he was silly when they found out he kissed a frog

_____

_____

62. Frogs dont want kids kissing them.

_____

63–64. The newspaper uses bold type alliteration and humour to capture the readers attention

_____

_____

65. There are a number of symptoms associated with salmonella including sickness diarrhoea and vomiting.

_____

_____

/9

Draw lines to match the words in the left-hand column to the synonyms on the right.

66. Magnificent   Insist

67. Claimed   Believed

68. Thought   Concern   /5

69. Demand   Stated

70. Worry   Marvellous

/70

PAPER 4

'Charles Dickens: The Early Years'

Charles John Huffam Dickens was born on 7th February, 1812 to John and Elizabeth. His
father was a naval pay clerk in their hometown of Portsmouth, England. He was one of eight
children and the eldest boy. Two of his younger siblings, Alfred and Harriet, died in infancy. This
was not uncommon in a time that had a child mortality rate where twenty per cent of children
died by the age of five. When Charles was five, the family moved to Chatham in Kent where   5
they remained for a further five years. Although a sickly child, up until the age of ten, Dickens
described his childhood as idyllic; he read avidly, explored the natural world and relished the
freedom his parents offered. John Dickens earned enough to enrol Charles into William Giles's
School, in Chatham, where he received a private education. At the age of 10, the Dickens family
moved to Camden Town in London due to his father's relocation for the Naval Pay Office.   10

The final move to Camden marked the end of Charles's tranquil childhood. His father was
fond of the good life; entertaining, socialising and borrowing beyond his means to maintain
a genteel position in society. He has been described as "a jovial opportunist with no money
sense", somewhat unfortunate given his employment in the Naval Pay Office. Thirteen days
after Charles's twelfth birthday, John Dickens was arrested and imprisoned for unpaid debts;   15
he owed the sum of £40.00 and 10 shillings to James Kerr, a baker. Although the entire
contents of the Dickens family house were sold, they could not raise the money to repay the
debt. John decided that Charles should stay in lodgings with an elderly family friend, Mrs
Roylance, whilst the rest of the family, with the exception of the eldest sister Fanny, were
moved to Marshelsea Debtor's Prison because it provided a better standard of living than   20
they would have otherwise. Debtors had to remain at the Marshelsea until they had repaid
their debts, but because they were imprisoned, debtors could not actually earn anything. As a
result, many debtors died in prison.

For three months, Charles was alone in a vast city, torn from his family, cold and near starving.
To pay for his board and meals, Charles started work at a boot-blacking factory. He had to walk   25
a gruelling four miles to the factory and four miles back, six days a week. For ten long hours a
day, he would paste labels on jars of shoe polish. He earned six shillings a week. On return to
his lodging, his evening meal would be typically meagre, only bread and cheese. The working
conditions in the factory were dire; rat-infested, dirty and unfit for adults, let alone children who
were considered cheap labour. The greatest pain for Charles was not the appalling physical   30
conditions, but the crippling despair he felt at being separated from his family. He was only
re-united with them during Sunday visits with Fanny, who was fortunate enough to be studying
at the Royal Academy for Music.

These early experiences in Dickens's childhood proved to be a rich source of material for his
writing. Many of the people who made an impact, whether negative or positive, on Dickens's   35
early years, reappear in his stories, which are so popular today that over 180 films and
television series have been made from them.

Read the passage then answer the following questions.

Write a definition for each of these words.

1. autobiography _____

2. biography _____

3. jovial _____

4. genteel _____

5. creditor _____

/5

Label the following pronouns as **personal, reflexive, demonstrative** or **indefinite**.

6. I _____

7. anyone _____

8. herself _____

9. you _____

10. myself _____

11. he _____

12. those _____

13. we _____

14. they _____

/10

15. everyone _____

Circle the correct word or phrase to complete each sentence.

16. The debtors' prison allows prisoners to receive visits from _____ families.

    their   they're   there

17. We were horrified to see the terrible conditions _____ were working in.

    they're children   your child   the children

18. He needed to _____ family regularly.

    see his   sea his   see them

19. They needed someone to pay off their debts and save them, but _____ did not appear very quickly.

    a such person   such a person   such person

20. Dickens's novel is very critical of the social conditions at the time and is

    clearly _____.

    intended to   intended   intended to be

/5

Answer these questions.

21. How many of the Dickens children moved to Chatham in Kent? _____

22. Why do you think the child mortality rate was so high when Charles was born?

_____

23. What year did the Dickens family move to Camden Town? _____

/3

List three things that made Charles's early childhood idyllic.

24. _____

25. _____

26. _____

/3

List three reasons which explain why John Dickens got into debt.

27. _____

28. _____

29. _____

/3

Answer these questions.

30. What month and year was John Dickens arrested for debt? _____

31. Why did many debtors die in prison?

_____

_____

32. How many of the Dickens's children went to prison? _____

33. Why did the family move to Marshelsea Debtor's Prison?

_____

_____

34. Explain why you think that Mrs Dickens did not get a job to help pay for the debts.

_____

_____

35. Why did the factory employ children?

_____

_____

36. What do you think Charles found most difficult about the time his family was in prison?

_____

_____

37. Who do you think is responsible for Charles's difficulties?

_____

38. Explain your answer to question 37.

_____

_____

39. Why do you think Fanny was fortunate to be studying at the Royal Academy of Music?

_____

_____

40. Explain whether you think that Charles Dickens's early experiences benefited him.

_____

_____

/11

> Circle the best synonym for the word in bold in each phrase below.

41. 'child **mortality** rate where twenty per cent of children died by the age of five'

death   living   birth

42. 'Dickens describes his childhood as **idyllic**'

sad   precious   peaceful

43. '**relished** the freedom his parents offered'

disliked   delighted   participated

44. 'a **jovial** opportunist with no money sense'

unhappy   happy   miserable

45. 'his evening meal would be typically **meagre**, only bread and cheese'

cold   large   small

/5

Underline the **temporal connectives** in the following phrases.

46. When Charles was five, the family moved to Chatham in Kent where they remained for a further five years.

47. Although a sickly child, up until the age of ten, Dickens describes his childhood as idyllic.

48. Debtors had to remain at the Marshelsea until they had repaid their debts.

49. For three months, Charles was alone in a vast city, torn from his family, cold and near starving.

50. On return to his lodging, his evening meal would be typically meagre, only bread and cheese.

/5

Imagine you are interviewing Charles Dickens.
Write questions for the following answers.

51. Question: _____

   Answer: My birthday is February 7th, 1812.

52. Question: _____

   Answer: I call them Mother and Father but their names are John and Elizabeth.

53. Question: _____

   Answer: My brother, Alfred, died when he was one. We were very sad to lose him but it was quite common then.

54. Question: _____

   Answer: Until I was ten, I had the happiest childhood you could imagine.

55. Question: _____

   Answer: I loved to read and still do.

/5

Rewrite the following sentences so that they are in the present tense and first person.

56. His father was fond of the good life.

_____

57. He would have to walk four miles to the factory and four miles back.

_____

_____

58. On return to his lodging, his evening meal would be typically meagre, only bread and cheese.

_____

_____

59. He saw them only on Sundays when he visited the prison with Fanny.

_____

_____

60. These early experiences in Dickens's childhood proved to be a rich source of material for his writing.

_____

_____

/5

Complete the words below using the clues to help you.

61. Go__ __ __ __ ment: the people who make the laws for the country

62. S__ __ r__ e: a text or a person that provides information

63. B __ __ s: a preference for a particular point of view, to be partial

64. Do__ __ ment: a formal piece of writing

65. D __ __ ry: a journal that records daily events

Using evidence from lines 24–33, find quotations
to support the following points.

66. The writer immediately encourages sympathy for Charles at the beginning of this
paragraph.

_____

_____

_____

67. The writer uses repetition to emphasise how difficult this period of life was for Dickens.

_____

_____

_____

68. The writer uses a cluster of three phrases to show the reader how awful the working
conditions were.

_____

_____

_____

69. A typical day for Dickens when he was a child was _____
_____ for ten hours a day.

70. The writer ends the paragraph with a sense of hope.

_____

_____

/5

/70

PAPER 5

'If' by Rudyard Kipling

IF you can keep your head when all about you
Are losing theirs and blaming it on you,
If you can trust yourself when all men doubt you,
But make allowance for their doubting too;
If you can wait and not be tired by waiting,   5
Or being lied about, don't deal in lies,
Or being hated, don't give way to hating,
And yet don't look too good, nor talk too wise.

If you can dream — and not make dreams your master;
If you can think — and not make thoughts your aim;   10
If you can meet with Triumph and disaster
And treat those two imposters just the same;
If you can bear to hear the truth you've spoken
Twisted by knaves to make a trap for fools,
Or watch the things you gave your life to, broken,   15
And stoop and build 'em up with worn-out tools;

If you can make one heap of all your winnings
And risk it on one turn of pitch-and-toss,
And lose, and start again at your beginnings
And never breathe a word about your loss;   20
If you can force your heart and nerve and sinew
To serve your turn long after they are gone,
And so hold on when there is nothing in you
Except the Will which says to them: 'Hold on!'

If you can talk with crowds and keep your virtue,   25
Or walk with Kings — nor lose the common touch,
If neither foes nor loving friends can hurt you,
If all men count with you, but none too much;
If you can fill the unforgiving minute
With sixty seconds' worth of distance run,   30
Yours is the Earth and everything that's in it,
And — which is more — you'll be a Man, my son!

Read the poem then answer the following questions.

Draw lines to match the quotations from the poem in the right-hand column to their explanations in the left-hand column.

1. I can remain calm when everyone else is panicking and pointing the finger at me.

'If you can bear to hear the truth you've spoken / Twisted by knaves to make a trap for fools'

2. I have confidence in myself even if other people do not.

'If you can talk with crowds and keep your virtue'

3. I do not take revenge on other people even if they treat me badly.

'Or watch the things you gave your life to, broken, / And stoop and build 'em up with worn-out tools'

4. I have ambition but I know it is not the most important thing in my life.

'And yet don't look too good, nor talk too wise.'

5. I believe in what I say and it doesn't matter if other people turn it against me.

'If you can trust yourself when all men doubt you'

6. I work hard for things but if they are damaged, I will simply start again with whatever I have left.

'If you can fill the unforgiving minute With sixty seconds' worth of distance run'

7. Even when I am exhausted, I will carry on.

'Or being lied about, don't deal in lies, Or being hated, don't give way to hating'

8. When I know that I am right, I will not boast about it.

'If you can force your heart and nerve and sinew / To serve your turn long after they are gone'

9. It doesn't matter whose celebrity company I am in, I will always be true to the ordinary person.

'IF you can keep your head when all about you / Are losing theirs and blaming it on you'

10. As a leader, I will always act honestly.

'Or walk with Kings — nor lose the common touch'

11. I make the most of every moment.

'If you can dream — and not make dreams your master'

/11

Write the correct synonym from the box for each of the words in bold in the sentences below.

muscle	rogues	victory	enemies	ruler
morality	frauds	distrust	spirit	

12. If you can trust yourself when all men **doubt** you _____

13. If you can dream — and not make dreams your **master** _____

14. If you can meet with **Triumph** and disaster _____

15. And treat those two **impostors** just the same _____

16. Twisted by **knaves** to make a trap for fools _____

17. If you can force your heart and nerve and **sinew** _____

18. Except the **Will** which says to them: 'Hold on!' _____

19. If you can talk with crowds and keep your **virtue** _____

20. If neither **foes** nor loving friends can hurt you _____

/9

State whether the conditional 'if' or 'when' in the following sentences suggests:

   a. Present real conditional that happens regularly

   b. Present real conditional that happens less frequently

   c. Present unreal conditional

   d. Present real conditional

21. If all men count with you, but none too much _____

22. If I won the lottery, I would give it all to charity. _____

23. When the odds are down, I work even harder. _____

24. When my friends need me, I am always there. _____

25. If you can think — and not make thoughts your aim _____

26. If I am late home, I am grounded for a week. _____

27. When I am famous, I will remember those who helped me. _____

28. When I go on holiday, I wear sunscreen. _____

29. If I finish my homework on time, I can play on the computer. _____

30. If neither foes nor loving friends can hurt you _____

/10

Complete this summary table for each of the verses in the poem.

31–42.

	Key Point	Evidence in the form of a quote	Explanation
Verse 1			
Verse 2			
Verse 3			
Verse 4			

/12

Write which characteristic from the box is suggested by each of the following lines from the poem.

humility	endurance	wisdom	determination
dignity	calmness	empathy	patience	graciousness

43. Lines 1 and 2 _____

44. Line 5 _____

45. Line 8 _____

46. Lines 11 and 12 _____

47. Lines 15 and 16 _____

48. Lines 17–20 _____

49. Lines 23–24 _____

50. Line 26 _____

51. Line 28 _____

/9

Fill in the blanks in these sentences.

52. The main feature of the poem is the repeated use of the _____ conditional 'if'.

53. The poet uses this feature at the start of each verse of the poem which makes the poem

_____.

54. The effect is an _____ in tension because we want to find out what will happen.

55. The tension is released in the _____ verse when the poet reveals the answer.

56. The rhyme scheme in the _____ verse is different to the other three verses.

57. The description of Triumph and Disaster as 'imposters' is an example of

_____.

58. There are a number of _____ phrases in the poem such as 'Triumph and Disaster' and 'Walk with Kings — nor lose the common touch'.

59. The poem appeals _____ to the reader through the repeated use of the personal pronoun 'you'.

60. The description of the 'unforgiving minute' is an example of _____.

61. This description of time is effective because you _____ turn back time and it will carry on regardless of what you may want.

62. The poet's use of contractions such as 'don't' gives a tone of _____ to the poem.

63. The final line of the poem reveals that the wise words are being passed from

_____ to son.

64. The poem could be viewed as a _____ to life.

65. The recommendations about how to behave in the poem are not for superheroes but are

all _____.

66. The capitalisation of 'Will' indicates that the poet is referring to a _____ source of strength.

67. Although the poem was published in 1909 it is still relevant for today's

_____.

68. The advice in the poem is equally relevant to _____ as well as boys.

69. The poem was voted the nation's favourite poem in 1995 which tells you that it still

_____ people years after it was written.

70. The line of the poem I like best is _____

/19

because _____

_____

/70

PAPER 6

From The Sunday Times
February 14, 2010

Children paid to plug junk food on Facebook and Bebo

Kate Walsh and Kevin Dowling

Children are being given rewards to promote Fanta, Nintendo and other products to their Facebook friends in a controversial form of stealth marketing.

In some cases children as young as seven have been offered the chance to become "mini-marketeers" to plug brands by casually dropping them into postings and conversations on social networking sites.   5

They can earn the equivalent of £25 a week for their online banter — sometimes promoting things that they may not even like. Among the products being pushed are soft drinks, including Sprite and Dr Pepper, Cheestrings and a Barbie-themed MP3 player. Record labels are also using the marketing technique to promote performers such as Lady Gaga. Multinational companies are using specialist marketing firms to recruit the children after they were   10
banned from setting up fake websites and blogs to target young customers directly.

"It's a tragedy," said Frank Furedi, professor of sociology at Kent University. "What should be an area where kids just hang out with each other and message each other now becomes an extension of the shopping mall."

The marketing agencies advise their young recruits to target different sets of online friends   15
with different brands and coach them to sound "natural and unrehearsed".

Molly, a 12-year-old from Cambridge who did not want to give her full name, has recently applied to a Leeds-based agency called Dubit Insider to promote products through Facebook and Bebo accounts that link her to almost 200 friends.

"I heard about it from one of my Facebook friends," she said. "They're going to pay me £25   20
a week [in gift vouchers] just to say stuff online about sweets and games. They also said they would send me lots of cool samples in the post."

Dubit has used so-called "brand ambassadors", ranging from seven to university age, to plug drinks produced by the Coca-Cola Company, Cheestrings, made by Kerry Foods, Nintendo and the Barbie MP3 player.   25

On its website, Dubit says children should promote "key campaign messages to friends, both on and offline" by posting comments on message boards, through instant messaging, such as MSN, and by hosting parties where product samples are distributed.

They should prepare their product pitch by "thinking deeply about how you would describe it to your best friend ... Write down the key points in your own words and make sure it doesn't   30
sound too rehearsed. Be natural; be you".

The website adds: "Don't start a chat about the project — it's best to look for natural opportunities to drop it into the conversation."

Recruits are rewarded with vouchers that can be redeemed at most high street stores — although they must first prove how much effort they have put into plugging products. Evidence includes screenshots and links to their online work and photographs of any other activities, which Dubit passes on to clients.   35

Another marketing agency, in4merz.com, uses a network of 10,000 youths, aged 11-21, to promote pop artists including Lady Gaga, Jonas Brothers, Alexandra Burke, Sugababes and Pixie Lott on behalf of record labels.   40

The agency encourages the youngsters to produce YouTube videos to help promote artists to their friends.

"We're turning them into mini-marketeers," Clare Hudson, founder of in4merz.com, said. She claimed that up to 100 children a day were signing up to her network, overseen by a team of 15 online supervisors. Members are rewarded with points for their promotional activities, which can be exchanged for music-related gifts.   45

Jemma, 12, from Stratford, east London, who has been working for the agency since last June, said: "Sometimes, like on a 50-point mission, they'll have something about, say the Jonas Brothers, and because I want to get the 50 points, I'll promote them even though I'm not a massive fan."   50

A spokesman for Coca-Cola said its brand ambassadors recruited through Dubit were over 16 and were told to make it clear they were being paid to promote the company's brands. A spokesman for Kerry Foods said its campaign to promote Cheestrings was a trial. Robin Hilton, Dubit's marketing director, said of his recruits: "They must make people aware they are involved in a project if talking about a product or brand. Anyone under the age of 16 must have explicit verbal parental consent to take part."   55

Read the article then answer the following questions.

Draw lines to match the words from the article in the left-hand column with the definitions in the right-hand column.

1. Controversy   representative

2. Networking   very clear

3. Technique   exchange for goods

4. Extension   lengthy argument

5. Promote   method

6. Ambassador   organised support to share information and services

7. Campaign   task or assignment

8. Redeem   project to achieve an aim

9. Mission   addition

10. Explicit   advertise

/10

Complete these sentences by filling in the gaps in the words, using the clue in brackets to help you.

11. There are numerous possible co___s___qu___n___ ___s (results) of using children to market products.

12. So___ ___ ___logi___ts (academics who study society) have conducted research into the link between advertising and social networking sites.

13. A long term ev___l___ at___ ___ n (assessment) of the relationship will be published shortly.

14. Advertising agencies are keen to fu___ ___il (complete) their promises to multinational companies.

15. Marketing companies will often give gen___r___ ___sly (charitably) to successful brand ambassadors.

16. Positive messages about brands could be in ci___c___lat___ ___ n (distributed) to hundreds of children through social networking sites in a matter of minutes.

17. The ac__i__v__ m__ nt (accomplishment) of plugging products brings voucher rewards for the best marketers.

18. New products or services are often dep__nd__nt (reliant) upon positive word of mouth to be successful.

19. Parents must offer their verbal aut__ __ris__t__ __n (permission) for children to take part in plugging brands.

20. The te__ __n__log__ __al (scientific) advancements of the age suggest that advertising will become increasingly sophisticated.

/10

Draw lines to match the types of adverbs in the left-hand column to the examples in the right-hand column.

21. Manner   too

22. Place   often

23. Time   cool

24. Frequency   personally

25. Degree   only

26. Interrogation   casually

27. Attitude   however

28. Viewpoint   why

29. Linking   here

30. Addition or deduction   recently

/10

For each adverb type, write whether it usually comes at the beginning, middle or end of a sentence.

31. Manner   _____

32. Place   _____

33. Time   _____

34. Frequency _____

35. Degree _____

36. Interrogation _____

37. Attitude _____

38. Viewpoint _____

39. Linking _____

40. Addition or deduction _____

/10

Underline the word(s) or phrase(s) in each sentence that
suggest opposition to children marketing brands.

41. 'In some cases children as young as seven have been offered the chance to become
"mini-marketeers".'

42. '...to plug brands by casually dropping them into postings and conversations on social
networking sites.'

43. 'They can earn the equivalent of £25 a week for their online banter — sometimes
promoting things that they may not even like.'

44. 'Among the products being pushed are soft drinks, including Sprite and Dr Pepper,
Cheestrings and a Barbie-themed MP3 player.'

45. 'Multinational companies are using specialist marketing firms to recruit the children
after they were banned from setting up fake websites and blogs to target young
customers directly.'

/5

Answer these questions.

46–47. Which two words in the following sentence suggest that there is a problem with children
being given rewards to promote products?

'Children are being given rewards to promote Fanta, Nintendo and other products to
their Facebook friends in a controversial form of stealth marketing.'

Word 1: _____

Word 2: _____

48. Does the article present the first quotation as supporting or opposing the marketing technique of employing children to promote products?

_____

49. Why do you think that Molly, a 12-year-old from Cambridge, did not want to give her full name?

_____

50. How do we know that the comment 'In some cases children as young as seven have been offered the chance to become "mini-marketeers"… ' is accurate? Find a quotation to support your answer.

_____

_____

51. Does Coca-Cola use brand ambassadors as young as seven? Provide evidence.

_____

_____

52. Find a quotation from an employee from Dubit that **contradicts** the following statement about how children should promote key campaign messages:

'Write down the key points in your own words and make sure it doesn't sound too rehearsed.'

_____

_____

/7

Find five quotations to support the point that using children to promote products is a form of 'stealth marketing'.

53. _____

54. _____

55. _____

56. _____

57. _____

/5

Find five quotations to explain why children agree to promote products.

58. _____

59. _____

60. _____

61. _____

62. _____ /5

Find five quotations that marketing agents such as Dubit and in4merz.com use to advise children how to promote products.

63. _____

64. _____

65. _____

66. _____

67. _____ /5

Answer the following questions.

68. How are children paid for promoting products? _____

_____

69. What three examples of evidence must children provide in order to be paid?

_____

70. Find a child's quotation from the article that supports the claim that they are 'sometimes promoting things that they may not even like'. /3

_____

_____ /70

PAPER 7

'The Voice' by Thomas Hardy

Woman much missed, how you call to me, call to me,
Saying that now you are not as you were
When you had changed from the one who was all to me,
But as at first, when our day was fair.

Can it be you that I hear? Let me view you, then,   5
Standing as when I drew near to the town
Where you would wait for me: yes, as I knew you then,
Even to the original air-blue gown!

Or is it only the breeze in its listlessness
Travelling across the wet mead to me here,   10
You being ever dissolved to wan wistlessness,
Heard no more again far or near?

Thus I; faltering forward,
Leaves around me falling,
Wind oozing thin through the thorn from norward,   15
And the woman calling.

> Read the poem then answer the following questions.

Choose the correct suffix or prefix from the box for each of the words below.

omni	ly	e-	tele	less	able	Neo-	micro	ese	ive

1. book   _____

2. chip   _____

3. present   _____

4. classical _____

5. scope   _____

6. treat   _____

7. care _____

8. attract _____

9. slow _____

10. Vietnam _____

/10

Suggest definitions for the following words from the poem.

11. wistlessness _____

12. listlessness _____

13. norward _____

14. faltering _____

15. mead _____

/5

Suggest synonyms for the words or phrases in bold in the sentences below.

16. The speaker **misses** the woman in the poem. _____

17. She wore an **original** blue gown. _____

18. The speaker hears the woman calling **all the time**. _____

19. The speaker feels **sorry** that the woman has died. _____

20. The speaker **says** that the woman meant everything to him. _____

/5

Write a sentence summarising each of the four verses in the poem.

21. Verse 1: _____

22. Verse 2: _____

_____

23. Verse 3: _____

24. Verse 4: _____

_____

/4

Answer the following questions.

25. Is the poem written in the first person, second person or third person?

_____

26. Why do you think Thomas Hardy chose to write the poem from this point of view?

_____

27–28. What two things does the speaker mistake the woman's voice for?

_____

29. Do you think the woman referred to in the poem is alive? _____

30–31. Find two lines from the poem to support your answer to question 29.

Line 1: _____

Line 2: _____

32. Which word identifies the extent of the speaker's loss? _____

/8

In the table below write a Y for yes or N for no to say whether each verse has references to the past, present or future.

33–44.

	Verse 1	Verse 2	Verse 3	Verse 4
Past				
Present				
Future				

/12

Answer these questions.

45. Which tense is most frequent in the poem: past, present or future? _____

46. Suggest a reason why this is the most frequent tense.

_____

47. Which tense is least frequent in the poem? _____

48. Suggest a reason why this is the least frequent tense.

_____ /4

Name the sound patterns in bold in the following quotations.

49. Woman **much missed**, how you call to me, call to me _____

50. Thus I; faltering forward _____

51. You being ever di**ss**olved to wan wistle**ssne ss** _____

52. Wind oozing **th**in **th**rough **the th**orn from norward _____ /4

Answer the following questions.

53. What is the significance of the imagery: 'Leaves around me falling.'?

_____

54. Why do you think the poet repeats the image of the woman calling in the first and the last lines only?

_____ /2

Identify the following lines as hopeful or sad, giving a reason for your answer.

55. 'But as at first, when our day was fair' is _____

56. This is because _____

57. 'Even to the original air-blue gown!' is _____

58. This is because _____

_____

59. 'Or is it only the breeze in its listlessness' is _____

60. This is because _____

_____

61. 'Travelling across the wet mead to me here,' is _____

62. This is because _____

_____

63. 'Wind oozing thin through the thorn from norward,' is _____

64. This is because _____

_____

/10

In the table below, put a tick in either the past, present or future column for each quotation from the poem.

	Past	Present	Future
65. 'Woman much missed, how you call to me, call to me,'			
66. 'But as at first, when our day was fair.'			
67. 'Can it be you that I hear?'			
68. 'yes, as I knew you then, Even to the original air-blue gown!'			
69. 'You being ever dissolved to wan wistlessness, Heard no more again far or near?'			

/5

70. Explain why the title of the poem is appropriate.

_____

/1

/70

PAPER 8

From The Times
July 25, 2006
Parents of cyber-bullies slapped with £1,000 fines
By Alexandra Blair, Education Correspondent

PARENTS of persistent school bullies could face fines of up to £1,000 if they fail to tackle
their children's behaviour.

The Government has issued tough new guidelines on cyber-bullying as research published
today shows that one in five pupils has been bullied via their mobile phone or the internet.
Under the guidelines, schools will have to monitor "all e-communications on the school site   5
or as part of school activities off-site". They will also have to update their anti-bullying policies
and teach pupils e-etiquette.

"No child should suffer the misery of bullying, online or offline, and we will support schools in
tackling it in cyberspace with the same vigilance as in the playground," said Jim Knight, the
Schools Minister.   10

"Every school should account for cyber-bullying in their compulsory anti-bullying policies, and
should take firm action where it occurs."

Mr Knight said that the Education and Inspections Bill would give teachers a "legal right to
discipline pupils" and enable them to take firm action on bullying.

Meanwhile, orders would force parents to tackle their child's persistent bullying and attend   15
parenting classes or face £1,000 fines.

Currently, pupils must be excluded once or suspended twice from school before their parents
face any fine.

According to recent estimates, almost two thirds of teenagers aged 13 to 17 have home pages
on networking sites, where they post photographs or chat with friends.   20

A survey for the Anti-Bullying Alliance — involving 92 pupils from 14 London schools — found
that a fifth had been victims of bullying by text, email or phone at least once or twice in the
past two months.

"Happy slapping" — in which an attack on a victim is videoed via mobile phone — was
considered to be the worst form of cyber-bullying, while chatroom and instant-message   25
bullying were considered less harmful than traditional forms.

One third of the victims said that they did not report bullying incidents.

The study was led by Peter Smith, Professor of Psychology at Goldsmiths College, London. He
said: "Ten years ago, psychologists thought of aggression in verbal or physical terms, which
traditionally was a male domain. But cyber-bullying is more akin to relational or indirect bullying,   30
such as spreading rumours, where girls are more likely to get involved."

For phone abuse, the Government recommends that victims turn off incoming SMS for a few days, change their phone number and do not reply to text or video messages. Text harassment is punishable by up to six months in prison.

HOW PHONE VICTIMS CAN GET HELP   35
Tesco Mobile has a 24-hour service for young people being cyber-bullied. Text "bully" to 60000 to receive advice and support. The cost of the texts is donated to NCH, the children's charity. BT has a freephone number offering recorded advice — 0800 666 700. People can also call free on 150 for personal advice. If the problem continues, a BT bureau is available on 0900 661 441 during office hours. It deals with malicious and nuisance calls and   40
may suggest tracing future calls or changing numbers. O2's nuisance call bureau can be contacted by e-mail at ncb@o2.com or by contacting its customer service department on 0870 5214 000. O2 also has online leaflets at www.O2.com/cr/network_safety.asp. Vodafone offers its RespondPlus service. An operator answers calls, takes messages and texts them to customers. Visit www.vodafone.co.uk.

> Read the article then answer the following questions using your own words as far as possible rather than words from the text.

1. Why might parents face fines of up to £1,000?

   _____

2. Why has the government issued new guidelines on cyber-bullying?

   _____

3–5. According to the new guidelines, what three responsibilities do schools now have in relation to cyber bullying?

   Responsibility 1: _____

   Responsibility 2: _____

   Responsibility 3: _____

6. What new legal right do teachers have according to the Education and Inspections Bill?

   _____

7. What is the alternative to a parent paying a fine for £1,000?

   _____

8. What is thought to be the worst form of cyber-bullying? _____

9. One third of how many victims said that they "did not report bullying incidents"?

_____

10. What is the most serious punishment for text harassment?

_____

/10

Unscramble these letters to make a word relating to ICT terminology.

11. Cross rope _____

12. Invite trace _____

13. Cent coo inn _____

14. Dial mum tie _____

15. Entice far _____

16. Maybe get _____

17. Desert phase _____

18. Dig crate _____

19. Abate sad _____

20. Prom rag _____

/10

Suggest synonyms for the words in bold.

21. They will also have to update their anti-bullying policies and teach pupils

    e-etiquette. _____

22. 'we will support schools in tackling it in cyberspace with the same **vigilance** as in the

    playground,' _____

23. 'Every school should account for cyber-bullying in their **compulsory** anti-bullying

    policies ...' _____

24. 'Ten years ago, psychologists thought of **aggression** in verbal or physical terms …'

_____

25. 'But cyber-bullying is more **akin** to relational or indirect bullying…'

_____

/5

Underline the word that makes the following sentences persuasive and state whether it is used as a noun or an adjective.

26. PARENTS of persistent school bullies could face fines of up to £1,000 if they fail to tackle their children's behaviour. _____

27. The Government has issued tough new guidelines on cyber-bullying as research published today shows that one in five pupils has been bullied via their mobile phone or the internet. _____

28. "No child should suffer the misery of bullying, online or offline…" _____

29. "Every school should account for cyber-bullying in their compulsory anti-bullying policies, and should take firm action where it occurs." _____

30. "Happy slapping" — in which an attack on a victim is videoed via mobile phone — was considered to be the worst form of cyber-bullying. _____

/5

Rewrite the following sentences changing them from the **active voice** to the **passive voice** or from the passive to the active.

31. PARENTS of persistent school bullies could face fines of up to £1,000 if they fail to tackle their children's behaviour.

_____

_____

32. Under the guidelines, schools will have to monitor 'all e-communications on the school site or as part of school activities off-site'.

_____

_____

33. 'Every school should account for cyber-bullying in their compulsory anti-bullying policies.'

_____

_____

34. Currently, pupils must be excluded once or suspended twice from school before their parents face any fine.

_____

_____

35. One third of the victims said that they did not report bullying incidents.

_____

36. Why do you think most of the sentences in the article are written in the active voice?

_____ /6

Summarise the argument that parents of cyber-bullies should be fined £1000.

Why are parents responsible?

37. Point: _____

38. Evidence or example: _____

39. Explanation: _____

What can they do to help schools monitor e-communications?

40. Point: _____

41. Evidence or example: _____

42. Explanation: _____

How can parents encourage children to talk to them about bullying or being bullied?

43. Point: _____

44. Evidence or example: _____

45. Explanation: _____

/9

Give three examples of e-communication.

46. _____

47. _____

48. _____

/3

Answer these questions.

49. Why is it the school's responsibility to monitor 'all e-communications on the school site or as part of school activities off-site'?

_____

50–52. List three potential difficulties of this level of monitoring.

Difficulty 1: _____

Difficulty 2: _____

Difficulty 3: _____

53–55. For each of the three potential difficulties you have thought of, suggest how the school might be able to overcome them.

Solution 1: _____

Solution 2: _____

Solution 3: _____

56. Why must schools teach pupils e-etiquette?

_____

57–59. Provide three suggestions that a school might deliver to its pupils on the subject of e-etiquette.

Suggestion 1: _____

Suggestion 2: _____

/11

Suggestion 3: _____

60. Have teachers always had the legal right to discipline pupils? Explain your answer.

_____

_____

61. Why do you think the government has given such importance to reducing instances of cyber-bullying?

_____

62. Why will the incidents of bullying be higher than reported in the article?

_____

63. Do you agree with the statement that '"Happy slapping" is considered to be the worst form of cyber-bullying, while chatroom and instant-message bullying were considered less harmful than traditional forms.'? Give a reason for your answer.

_____

_____

64. According to Professor Smith, how have psychologists had to change their view about bullying?

_____

65. Why do you think the article ends with the sentence 'Text harassment is punishable by up to six months in prison.'?

_____

66. Explain why the headline is effective.

_____

67. What type of reader is the article aimed at? Explain your answer.

_____

_____

68. Why is the headline of the sub-article 'HOW PHONE VICTIMS CAN GET HELP' written in capitals?

_____

69. How would you improve the layout of the sub-article?

_____

70. Who do you think the article suggests is ultimately responsible for children who are cyber-bullies? Explain your answer.

_____

/11

_____

/70

PAPER 9

'White Fang' by Jack London

CHAPTER I — THE TRAIL OF THE MEAT

Dark spruce forest frowned on either side the frozen waterway. The trees had been stripped by a recent wind of their white covering of frost, and they seemed to lean towards each other, black and ominous, in the fading light. A vast silence reigned over the land. The land itself was a desolation, lifeless, without movement, so lone and cold that the spirit of it was not even that of sadness. There was a hint in it of laughter, but of a laughter more terrible than any sadness — a laughter that   5
was mirthless as the smile of the sphinx, a laughter cold as the frost and partaking of the grimness of infallibility. It was the masterful and incommunicable wisdom of eternity laughing at the futility of life and the effort of life. It was the Wild, the savage, frozen-hearted Northland Wild.

But there *was* life, abroad in the land and defiant. Down the frozen waterway toiled a string of wolfish dogs. Their bristly fur was rimed with frost. Their breath froze in the air as it left their   10
mouths, spouting forth in spumes of vapour that settled upon the hair of their bodies and formed into crystals of frost. Leather harness was on the dogs, and leather traces attached them to a sled which dragged along behind. The sled was without runners. It was made of stout birch-bark, and its full surface rested on the snow. The front end of the sled was turned up, like a scroll, in order to force down and under the bore of soft snow that surged like a   15
wave before it. On the sled, securely lashed, was a long and narrow oblong box. There were other things on the sled — blankets, an axe, and a coffee-pot and frying-pan; but prominent, occupying most of the space, was the long and narrow oblong box.

In advance of the dogs, on wide snowshoes, toiled a man. At the rear of the sled toiled a second man. On the sled, in the box, lay a third man whose toil was over, — a man whom the Wild had   20
conquered and beaten down until he would never move nor struggle again. It is not the way of the Wild to like movement. Life is an offence to it, for life is movement; and the Wild aims always to destroy movement. It freezes the water to prevent it running to the sea; it drives the sap out of the trees till they are frozen to their mighty hearts; and most ferociously and terribly of all does the Wild harry and crush into submission man — man who is the most restless of life, ever in revolt   25
against the dictum that all movement must in the end come to the cessation of movement.

But at front and rear, unawed and indomitable, toiled the two men who were not yet dead. Their bodies were covered with fur and soft-tanned leather. Eyelashes and cheeks and lips were so coated with the crystals from their frozen breath that their faces were not discernible. This gave them the seeming of ghostly masques, undertakers in a spectral world at the funeral of some   30
ghost. But under it all they were men, penetrating the land of desolation and mockery and silence, puny adventurers bent on colossal adventure, pitting themselves against the might of a world as remote and alien and pulseless as the abysses of space.

They travelled on without speech, saving their breath for the work of their bodies. On every side was the silence, pressing upon them with a tangible presence. It affected their minds as the   35
many atmospheres of deep water affect the body of the diver. It crushed them with the weight of unending vastness and unalterable decree. It crushed them into the remotest recesses of their own minds, pressing out of them, like juices from the grape, all the false ardours and

exaltations and undue self-values of the human soul, until they perceived themselves finite and
small, specks and motes, moving with weak cunning and little wisdom amidst the play and   40
inter-play of the great blind elements and forces.

An hour went by, and a second hour. The pale light of the short sunless day was beginning to
fade, when a faint far cry arose on the still air. It soared upward with a swift rush, till it reached
its topmost note, where it persisted, palpitant and tense, and then slowly died away. It might
have been a lost soul wailing, had it not been invested with a certain sad fierceness and hungry 45
eagerness. The front man turned his head until his eyes met the eyes of the man behind. And
then, across the narrow oblong box, each nodded to the other.

A second cry arose, piercing the silence with needle-like shrillness. Both men located the
sound. It was to the rear, somewhere in the snow expanse they had just traversed. A third and
answering cry arose, also to the rear and to the left of the second cry.   50

"They're after us, Bill," said the man at the front.

Read the passage then answer the following questions.

For each of these questions you should provide a supporting quote and comment on the
language used.

1–3. Where is the story set? _____

Supporting quote: _____

Comment on language: _____

4–6. How does the author present the environment? _____

Supporting quote: _____

Comment on language: _____

7–9. What is the conflict presented in the first paragraph of the story? _____

Supporting quote: _____

Comment on language: _____

10–12. In the second paragraph, how does the writer present the dogs?

_____

Supporting quote: _____

Comment on language: _____

13–15. What other signs of life are offered in the third paragraph? _____

Supporting quote: _____

Comment on language: _____

16–18. How does the author continue to emphasise the conflict between life and the environment

in the third paragraph? _____

Supporting quote: _____

Comment on language: _____

19–21. What do you think is in the long oblong box? _____

Supporting quote: _____

Comment on language: _____

22–24. How does London describe the men in the fourth paragraph that connects them to the

long oblong box? _____

Supporting quote: _____

Comment on language: _____

25–27. In the fifth paragraph, what effect does the silence have on the state of the men?

_____

Supporting quote: _____

Comment on language: _____

28–30. In the sixth paragraph, what noise causes the men to nod to each other?

_____

Supporting quote: _____

Comment on language: _____

31–33. How do the noises at the end of the extract change the mood of the story?

_____

Supporting quote: _____

Comment on language: _____   /33

Answer these questions.

34. Who does London present as more powerful in this extract, the Wild or human beings?

_____

35. What does the opening of the book suggest will happen to everyone who lives in the Wild?

_____   /2

Match each word in the box to its correct definition and write which line the word appears in.

desolation	mirthless	infallibility	futility
indomitable	prominent	toil	dictum
cessation	spectral	colossal	tangible
ardour	exaltations	palpitant	traversed

36. feeling of extreme happiness _____

37. large and projecting _____

38. a well-known saying _____

39. never make a mistake _____

40. move across an area _____

41. extremely large _____

42. stop _____

43. uninhabited _____

44. irregular heartbeat due to fear or anxiety _____

45. without joy _____

46. work _____

47. pointless action _____

48. brave _____

49. ghostly _____

50. able to be touched _____

51. intense emotion _____

/16

Identify the literary techniques being used in the following extracts from the text.

52. 'Dark spruce forest frowned on either side the frozen waterway.' _____

53. 'A laughter that was mirthless as the smile of the sphinx.' _____

54. 'It was the masterful and incommunicable wisdom of eternity laughing at the futility of life and the effort of life.' _____

55. 'The front end of the sled was turned up, like a scroll…' _____

56. 'On the sled, securely lashed, was a long and narrow oblong box. There were other things on the sled — blankets, an axe, and a coffee-pot and frying-pan; but prominent, occupying most of the space, was the long and narrow oblong box.' _____

57. 'It is not the way of the Wild to like movement.' _____

58. 'It freezes the water to prevent it running to the sea; it drives the sap out of the trees till they are frozen to their mighty hearts; and most ferociously and terribly of all does the Wild harry and crush into submission man…' _____

59. '…undertakers in a spectral world at the funeral of some ghost…' _____

60. '…penetrating the land of desolation and mockery and silence…' _____

61. 'On every side was the silence, pressing upon them with a tangible presence.'

_____

62. '…pressing out of them, like juices from the grape…' _____

63. 'A second cry arose, piercing the silence with needle-like shrillness.' _____

/12

Answer these questions.

64. What is the most frequent literary technique used in the extract? _____

65. Explain why you think this is effective.

_____

66. Why do you think London delays the introduction of any human life form until line 19?

_____

67. Why do you think London introduces the dogs to the reader before the humans?

_____

68. Suggest why London keeps the reader in suspense about the characters' names until line 51.

_____

69. What do you think the chapter title 'The trail of the meat' refers to?

_____

/7

70. How does the opening chapter encourage you to read on?

_____

/70

PAPER 10

'King Lear' Act 1 scene 1. by William Shakespeare

KING LEAR

Meantime we shall express our darker purpose.
Give me the map there. Know that we have divided
In three our kingdom: and 'tis our fast intent
To shake all cares and business from our age;
Conferring them on younger strengths, while we   5
Unburthen'd crawl toward death. ...
...Tell me, my daughters, —
Since now we will divest us both of rule,
Interest of territory, cares of state, —
Which of you shall we say doth love us most?   10
That we our largest bounty may extend
Where nature doth with merit challenge. Goneril,
Our eldest-born, speak first.

GONERIL

Sir, I love you more than words can wield the matter;
Dearer than eye-sight, space, and liberty;   15
Beyond what can be valued, rich or rare;
No less than life, with grace, health, beauty, honour;
As much as child e'er loved, or father found;
A love that makes breath poor, and speech unable;
Beyond all manner of so much I love you.   20

CORDELIA

[Aside] What shall Cordelia do?
Love, and be silent.

LEAR

Of all these bounds, even from this line to this,
With shadowy forests and with champains rich'd,
With plenteous rivers and wide-skirted meads,   25
We make thee lady; to thine and Albany's issue.
Be this perpetual. What says our second daughter,
Our dearest Regan, wife to Cornwall? Speak.

REGAN

Sir, I am made
Of the self-same metal that my sister is,   30
And prize me at her worth. In my true heart
I find she names my very deed of love;
Only she comes too short: that I profess
Myself an enemy to all other joys,

	Which the most precious square of sense possesses;	35
	And find I am alone felicitate	
	In your dear highness' love.	

CORDELIA

[Aside] Then poor Cordelia!
And yet not so; since, I am sure, my love's
More richer than my tongue.   40

KING LEAR

To thee and thine hereditary ever
Remain this ample third of our fair kingdom;
No less in space, validity, and pleasure,
Than that conferr'd on Goneril. Now, our joy,
Although the last, not least; to whose young love   45
The vines of France and milk of Burgundy
Strive to be interess'd; what can you say to draw
A third more opulent than your sisters? Speak.

CORDELIA

Nothing, my lord.

KING LEAR

Nothing!   50

CORDELIA

Nothing.

KING LEAR

Nothing will come of nothing; speak again.

CORDELIA

Unhappy that I am, I cannot heave
My heart into my mouth; I love your majesty
According to my bond; no more nor less.   55

KING LEAR

How, how, Cordelia! Mend your speech a little.
Lest it may mar your fortunes.

CORDELIA

Good my lord,
You have begot me, bred me, loved me: I
Return those duties back as are right fit.   60
Obey you, love you and most honour you.
Why have my sisters' husbands, if they say
They love you all? Haply, when I shall wed,
That lord whose hand must take my plight shall carry
Half my love with him, half my care and duty: 65
Sure, I shall never marry like my sisters,
To love my father all.

KING LEAR

But goes thy heart with this?

CORDELIA

Ay, my good lord.

KING LEAR

So young, and so untender?   70

CORDELIA

So young, my lord, and true.

KING LEAR

Let it be so: thy truth, then, be thy dower:
For, by the sacred radiance of the sun,
The mysteries of Hecate, and the night;
By all the operation of the orbs   75
From whom we do exist, and cease to be;
Here I disclaim all my paternal care,
Propinquity and property of book,
And as a stranger to my heart and me
Hold thee, from this, for ever…   80

Read the extract from the play then answer the following questions.

Match each word in the box to its correct definition and write which line the word appears in.

conferred	unburdened	divest	bounty
wield	liberty	champains	meads
perpetual	profess	felicitate	hereditary
interess'd	bond	haply	heave
radiance	hecate	orbs	disclaim	opulent

1. Move something using a lot of effort _____

2. Find happiness _____

3. Open, flat countryside _____

4. Say something publicly and openly _____

5. Rich or ample _____

6. Happily _____

7. To take something away from somebody, like power or status _____

8. Bright, glowing light _____

9. Take away the load from someone _____

10. Round, spherical objects _____

11. To discuss something with someone _____

12. Freedom to choose, think or act _____

13. A serious promise _____

14. Grassy fields _____

15. A reward _____

16. Refuse to have a connection with someone _____

17. Handed down through the generations _____

18. The Greek goddess of darkness _____

19. Interested in something _____

20. To use something _____

/20

Answer these questions.

21. What does King Lear want to do?

_____

22. Why does King Lear describe the purpose as 'darker'?

_____

/2

23–25. What three reasons does King Lear give for giving up his kingdom? Use your own words.

Reason 1: _____

Reason 2: _____

Reason 3: _____

26. What is the important question that King Lear asks at the beginning of the scene?

_____

27. How many times does King Lear demand an answer to the important question in this

extract? _____

28–30. What three things does King Lear claim to give up?

Item 1: _____

Item 2: _____

Item 3: _____

/8

Answer these questions.

31. How will the kingdom be divided? _____

32. How many daughters does King Lear have? _____

33. Write the daughters in order of age, beginning with the youngest daughter.

_____

34. What is Cordelia's first line to her father, King Lear?

_____

35. Who is Albany?

_____

36. Who is Cornwall?

_____

37. Which two men are interested in marrying Cordelia?

_____

38. What does Cordelia say will happen when she gets married?

_____

39. How many opportunities does King Lear give Cordelia to change her answer?

_____

40. Explain the effect of the pause in the middle and at the end of line 7.

_____

41. Why do you think Goneril begins her speech with 'Sir' instead of father?

_____

42. Why does Shakespeare give Goneril so many pauses in her speech?(lines 14–20)

_____

43. Remind yourself of lines 41–48. List the words or phrases that suggest King Lear feels differently about Cordelia than he does about his other daughters.

_____

_____

/13

Answer the following questions in full sentences.

44. Explain the line 'A love that makes breath poor, and speech unable;' (line 19).

_____

_____

45. How does Shakespeare introduce the audience to Cordelia?

_____

_____

46. What do Cordelia's asides tell the audience about her character?

_____

_____

47. Why do you think King Lear asks Cordelia the important question last?

_____

_____

48. What does Regan mean when she says she agrees with her sister, 'Only she comes too short.'? (line 33).

_____

_____

49. What does King Lear suggest that Cordelia's share of the kingdom will be like?

_____

_____

50. What do you think King Lear feels at line 50?

_____

_____

51. What is the most interesting question that Cordelia asks that makes the audience question Goneril and Regan's answers?

_____

_____

52. How does King Lear finally respond to Cordelia's answer? (lines 72–80).

_____

_____

/9

Answer the following questions as if you were a director.

53. As a director, what action would you ask the actor playing King Lear to perform at line 2?

_____

54. As a director, what gesture would you ask the actor playing King Lear to do in line 79?

_____

/2

Identify the literary techniques used in the following lines and explain what they mean.

55. '…my love's / More richer than my tongue.'

Literary technique: _____

Explanation: _____

56. 'Obey you, love you and most honour you.'

Literary technique: _____

Explanation: _____

57. 'I cannot heave / My heart into my mouth;'

Literary technique: _____

Explanation: _____

58. 'You have begot me, bred me, loved me'

Literary technique: _____

Explanation: _____

/4

Identify two literary techniques in the following quote and explain them both.

'That lord whose hand must take my plight shall carry / Half my love with him, half my care and duty:'

59. Literary technique: _____

Explanation: _____

60. Literary technique: _____

Explanation: _____

/2

Answer the following questions in full sentences.

61. Do you think that dividing the kingdom is a good decision for a King to make? Explain your answer.

_____

_____

62. Do you believe Goneril when she says her love for King Lear makes her 'breath poor and speech unable'?

_____

_____

63. Does Regan get a better share of the kingdom than her sister? Explain your answer using a quotation.

_____

_____

64. What does Cordelia's second aside tell the audience about her character?

_____

_____

65. Explain why Cordelia answers King Lear's question with 'Nothing.'

_____

_____

66. What do Lear's responses to Cordelia's answer of 'nothing' tell the audience about his feelings for Cordelia?

_____

_____

67. How does Cordelia describe her feelings for her father?

_____

_____

68. How does this compare with the feelings that her sisters have claimed?

_____

_____

69. Why does Cordelia say she will never marry?

_____

_____

70. Who does Shakespeare encourage the audience to sympathise with?

_____

_____

/10

/70

active voice	a sentence where emphasis is placed on who carried out the action
aside	a line in drama that is spoken aloud but the other characters cannot hear it
bias	a preference for something
broadsheet	a large, serious newspaper
caption	a description of a picture or illustration
connective (temporal)	a word or phrase that joins two ideas or clauses together using time
contractions	a shortened word form
contradiction	to go against an idea
director	a person who leads the actors and tells them how they should act
italics	a type of font that slants the words
passive voice	a sentence where emphasis is placed on what happened
personification	to describe an object with human qualities
present real conditional	used when talking about something that is possible in real-life
present unreal conditional	used when talking about something that is imaginary
pronoun (reflexive)	a pronoun that refers to the person, e.g. *myself, herself, yourself*
pronoun (demonstrative)	a pronoun that refers to an object, e.g. *this*, *that*, *these*, *those*
pronoun (indefinite)	a pronoun that could refer to anything or anyone, e.g. *some*, *nobody*, *something*
slang	an informal and common way of speaking or writing
strapline	a sub-heading in an article
sub-article	a smaller article with a similar theme to the main article
subjective	something that is based on someone's point of view rather than facts or evidence
summary	a short version that contains only the key points
tabloid	a small newspaper with short, popular articles often written in an informal way

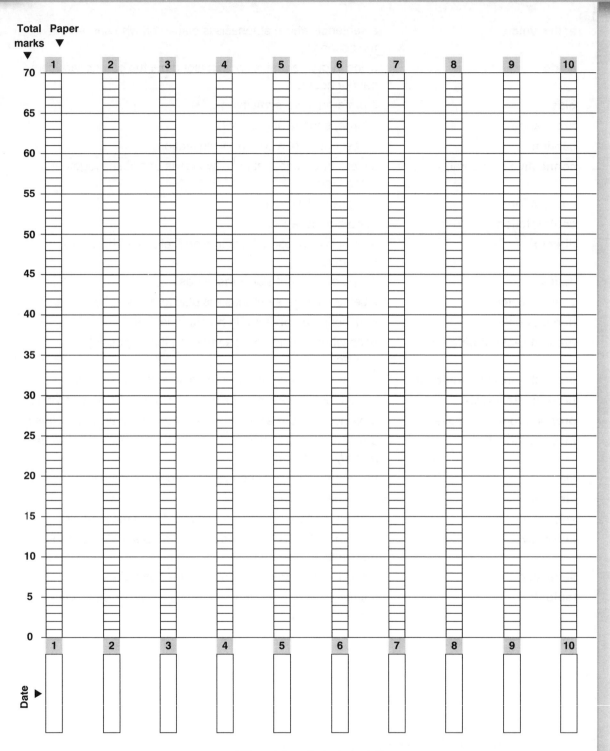

Total marks ▼ **Paper** ▼

Now colour in your score!

Date ▶

Answer booklet: KS3 English Levels 5–6

Please Note: Answers to questions which require explanation are given as guidance to the types of answers expected. Correct answers to these questions should contain the same meaning, but do not need to be word perfect with the example answers given.

Paper 1

1. third person
2. the country
3. working class
4. dusk
5. friends
6. George looks after Lennie which means that he cares for him and the author describes the two men as very different physically which makes the likelihood of them being related remote.
7. George and Lennie are planning to work on a ranch.
8–11. any four of the following: small, strong hands; dark face; restless eyes; sharp, strong features; slender arms; thin, bony nose.
12–15. any four of the following: huge, shapeless face, large pale eyes; wide, sloping shoulders; heavy hands.
16. brittle
17. thumped
18. appeared
19. titanic
20. uneasily
21. rapid
22. glumly
23. flicked
24. hugged
25. timorously
26. thrilled
27. complied
28–37. 'Okay-okay. <u>I</u> <u>will</u> tell <u>you</u> again. <u>I have not</u> got <u>anything</u> to do. I might <u>just</u> as well <u>spend</u> all my time <u>telling</u> you things and then you forget <u>them</u>, and I tell you again.'
38. George acts protectively towards Lennie ⟶ "for god's sakes don't drink so much … you gonna be sick."
39. Lennie tries to trick George ⟶ '"Ain't a think in my pocket," Lennie said cleverly'
40. George curses the busdriver ⟶ "Too God damn lazy to pull up"
41. Steinbeck opens the story with a description of dusk ⟶ "Evening of a hot day …"
42. Lennie has trouble remembering things ⟶ "So you forgot that awready did you?"
43. Correct sequence of events: 41, 38, 40, 42, 39.
44. George is looking out for Lennie.
45. Lennie looks to George for approval.
46. Lennie looks up to George and relies on him to show him how to act.
47. George knows that Lennie loses things so he looks after Lennie's important things.
48. Lennie does not think that anything can harm him.
49. Lennie tries to show George that he is good at something.
50. Lennie does not understand that keeping a dead mouse is unhygienic.
51. Lennie treats the dead mouse like a cuddly toy.
52. The short sentence shows how simple things like drinking water give Lennie joy.
53. The short sentence shows how frustrated George is that they had to walk four miles.
54. The short exclamation shows how important it is to Lennie that George believes him.
55. The short sentence reveals the shame that Lennie feels admitting to George that he has let him down again.
56. metaphor
57. simile
58. metaphor
59. simile
60. repetition
61. The story is set at the end of the day to show that George and Lennie are nearly at the end of their journey.
62. It gives us the impression that he is intelligent.
63. Lennie's behaviour gives us the impression that he has a simple, childlike innocence and that he cannot function on his own.
64. Steinbeck gives us the impression of a peaceful natural, idyllic setting undisturbed by human beings.
65. George feels responsible for Lennie and frustrated that he cannot remember things.
66. Lennie looks up to George and wants to please him the way a child wants to please their parent.
67. George feels angry that the bus driver tricked them into getting off the bus early.
68. George is worried because if Lennie doesn't remember what he is told, he could get them into trouble.
69. Lennie insists that he did not kill the mouse because he does not want George to think badly about him.
70. Answers will vary. Example answer: The story will have a sad ending because no matter how hard George tries to protect Lennie he cannot be there all of the time. This means that some time in the future, Lennie will get into trouble because he is so child-like and George will not be able to save him.

Paper 2

1. Biological
2. Energetic
3. Athletic
4. Fantastic/Fantastical
5. Critical
6. Grammatical
7. Artistic
8. Majestic/Majestical
9. Topical
10. Systematic/Systematical
11. tobacco
12. encouraged
13. coronary
14. addictive
15. unpolluted
16. Expectant
17. appearance
18. medicinal
19. knowledge
20. Participation
21. effect
22. persuasive
23. major
24. unnecessary
25. contact
26. broad
27. gather
28. promise
29. liability
30. forbid

31. useful

32. misunderstanding

33. Summarises the entire topic ⟶ Last paragraph

34. Most important point ⟶ Comes in the first paragraph

35. Outlines the entire topic ⟶ First paragraph

36. Repeats a word / phrase / ⟶ Links paragraphs
idea from a previous paragraph

37. Examples ⟶ Come after giving an opinion

38. Alternative viewpoint ⟶ Connectives such as however
/ although / whereas

39. A report shows that more than 22,000 children need medical help due to passive smoking.

40. Professor Briton says the report will influence policy about extending the smoking ban.

41. The report found that having parents who smoke increases passive smoking for children more than parents who do not smoke.

42. The report suggests that films with smoking should be classified as adult and there should be higher fines for selling cigarettes to those underage.

43. The report's 200 pages detail the impact of passive smoking on children.

44. There is a high cost to the NHS because of passive smoking.

45. Passive smoking is responsible for thousands of medical visits.

46. Passive smoking is responsible for one in five sudden infant deaths.

47. support

48. It suggests support for an extension to the ban because it identifies the effects of passive smoking.

49. support
50. oppose
51. support
52. support
53. support
54. support
55. support
56. support
57. support
58. support
59. support
60. support
61. strong
62. headline
63. young
64. cost
65. statistics
66. persuade
67. reduce
68. continues
69. emphasise
70. emotive

Paper 3

1. Fifty children caught salmonella in America after kissing a frog.

2. The Healthy Children Foundation advises parents to seek medical help for ill children.

3. An organisation, Freedom for Frogs, is concerned that people will respond to frogs negatively.

4. The newspaper is asking for people to sign their petition.

5. Answers will vary

6. Broadsheet

7. Tabloid

8. Broadsheet

9. Tabloid

10. Broadsheet

11. Tabloid

12. Tabloid

13. Tabloid

14. Tabloid

15. Broadsheet

16. "could reach phenomenal numbers."

17. "doing their own thing"

18. "There's no reason to hate frogs, just don't kiss them."

19. Don't trust this cheeky froggie!

20. Kissing sickness hits the States!

21. "Parents should call their doctor if their child is experiencing sickness, headaches or diarrhoea. With the correct treatment, usually antibiotics, they can fight the disease."

22. Fifty

23. To support the reason why children are kissing frogs.

24. To show the reader that boys have been kissing frogs and that parents have been surprised by their children's behaviour.

25. The article is humorous.

26. The style of the article is informal and the graphic and caption is comical.

27. No.

28. The statement in italics shows that they see the behaviour as silly.

29. To provide an alternative viewpoint for the frogs.

30. No.

31. They make frogs sound as if they are human.

32–34. sickness, diarrhoea, headaches

35. To show their readers that they are keen to support the campaign.

36. You would email the newspaper.

37. To emphasise the key message from the Healthy Children Foundation not to kiss frogs.

38–39. The picture is comical and personifies the frog which makes the article humorous rather than serious.

40. It captures the reader's attention by using rhyme and slang.

41. The reader will want to know how kissing can cause sickness.

42. fact
43. fact
44. opinion
45. fact
46. fact
47. opinion
48. opinion
49. fact
50. fact
51. opinion
52. bullet points
53. caption
54. headline
55. reporter
56. strapline

57. Tiffany said she kissed the frog because she wanted a prince.

58–60. I didn't want to get sick, I only wanted a prince.

61. Jack's friends thought he was silly when they found out he kissed a frog.

62. Frogs don't want kids kissing them.

63–64. The newspaper uses bold type, alliteration and humour to capture the readers' attention.

65. There are a number of symptoms associated with salmonella including sickness, diarrhoea and vomiting.

66. Magnificent ⟶ Marvellous

67. Claimed ⟶ Stated

68. Thought ⟶ Believed

69. Demand ⟶ Insist

70. Worry ⟶ Concern

Paper 4

1. An account of someone's life written by themselves

2. An account of someone's life written by someone else

3. Cheerful

4. Well-mannered / upper class

5. Somebody who is owed money

6. personal

7. indefinite

8. reflexive

9. personal
10. reflexive
11. personal
12. demonstrative
13. personal
14. personal
15. indefinite
16. their
17. the children
18. see his
19. such a person
20. intended to be
21. six (two had died in infancy)
22. the living conditions were much worse than they are today
23. 1822
24. freedom
25. reading
26. exploring the natural world
27. He lived beyond his means
28. He was fond of entertaining / socialising
29. He wanted to maintain his genteel lifestyle.
30. February 1824
31. They died in prison because they could not earn anything to repay their debt.
32. Four
33. Because the living conditions were better in prison than they would have experienced outside.
34. It would not have been considered to be appropriate for women of Mrs Dickens's class to work. / She had to look after the children.
35. Children were cheaper to employ than adults.
36. He would have found the separation the most difficult thing
37. His father, John Dickens
38. I think his father is responsible because he borrowed more than he could repay
39. She was fortunate because it meant that she had a way out of the situation.
40. They only benefited him because he made the most of them by writing about his experiences in stories.
41. death
42. peaceful
43. delighted
44. happy
45. small
46. When
47. up until
48. until
49. For three months
50. On return
51. When were you born?
52. Who are your parents?
53. What is your earliest saddest memory?
54. How would you describe your childhood?
55. What was your favourite activity when you were a child?
56. My father is fond of the good life.
57. I have to walk four miles to the factory and four miles back.
58. On return to my lodging, my evening meal is typically meagre, only bread and cheese.
59. I see them only on Sundays when I visit the prison with Fanny.
60. My early experiences in my childhood are a rich source of material for my writing.
61. Government
62. Source
63. Bias

64. Document
65. Diary
66. "Charles was alone in a vast city, torn from his family, cold and near starving."
67. "He would have to walk a gruelling four miles to the factory and a gruelling four miles back."
68. "rat-infested, dirty and unfit for adults"
69. "pasting labels on jars of shoe polish"
70. "He was only re-united with them"

Paper 5

1.	I can remain calm when everyone else is panicking and pointing the finger at me.	→	'IF you can keep your head when all about you Are losing theirs and blaming it on you,'
2.	I have confidence in myself even if other people do not	→	'If you can trust yourself when all men doubt you,'
3.	I do not take revenge on other people even if they treat me badly.	→	'Or being lied about, don't deal in lies, Or being hated, don't give way to hating,'
4.	I have ambition but I know it is not the most important thing in my life	→	'If you can dream – and not make dreams your master'
5.	I believe in what I say and it doesn't matter if other people turn it against me.	→	'If you can bear to hear the truth you've spoken Twisted by knaves to make a trap for fools,'
6.	I work hard for things but if they are damaged, I will simply start again with whatever I have left.	→	'Or watch the things you gave your life to, broken, And stoop and build 'em up with worn-out tools;'
7.	Even when I am exhausted, I will carry on.	→	'If you can force your heart and nerve and sinew To serve your turn long after they are gone,'
8.	When I know that I am right, I will not boast about it.	→	'And yet don't look too good, nor talk too wise.'
9.	It doesn't matter whose celebrity company I am in, I will always be true to the ordinary person.	→	'Or walk with Kings – nor lose the common touch,'
10.	As a leader, I will always act honesty	→	'If you can talk with crowds and keep your virtue,'
11.	I make the most of every moment.	→	'If you can fill the unforgiving minute With sixty seconds' worth of distance run,'

12. distrust
13. ruler
14. victory
15. frauds
16. rogues
17. muscle
18. spirit
19. moralities
20. enemies
21. c – present unreal conditional
22. c – present unreal conditional
23. d – present real conditional
24. d – present real conditional
25. c – present unreal conditional
26. d – present real conditional
27. c – present unreal conditional
28. a – present real condition that happens regularly
29. b – present real conditional that happens less regularly
30. c – present unreal conditional

3

The following is an example answer.

	Key Point	Evidence in the form of a quote	Explanation
Verse 1	The poem opens with suggestions for how to be self-confident and calm when other people disagree with you, without being arrogant.	'And yet don't look too good, nor talk too wise'	The last line of the verse encourages you to be balanced in your actions.
Verse 2	The second verse deals with how you face unknown difficulties in your life.	"If you can meet with Triumph and Disaster / And treat those two impostors just the same."	Kipling personifies victory and misfortune and suggests through the use of the word 'impostors' that following either would be foolish.
Verse 3	The third verse is about being determined in everything you do no matter what the outcome is.	'And so hold on when there is nothing in you'	The phrase 'hold on' is also repeated at the end of the last line, highlighting the importance of determination.
Verse 4	Kipling completes the poem with the revelation that the persona is a father giving advice to his son.	'And – which is more – you'll be a Man, my son.'	The capitalisation of 'Man' suggests that if someone is able to follow the advice in the poem they will attain a higher status than an ordinary man.

43. calmness
44. patience
45. humility
46. wisdom
47. dignity
48. endurance
49. determination
50. graciousness
51. empathy
52. unreal
53. cohesive
54. increase
55. final / last / fourth
56. first
57. personification
58. contrasting
59. directly
60. personification
61. cannot
62. informality
63. Father
64. guide
65. achievable
66. spiritual / higher / religious
67. society / children
68. girls
69. inspires
70. Example: The line of the poem I like best is the last line because it reveals the reward of following the advice of the poem.

Paper 6

1. Controversy ⟶ lengthy argument
2. Networking ⟶ organised support to share information and services
3. Technique ⟶ method
4. Extension ⟶ addition
5. Promote ⟶ advertise
6. Ambassador ⟶ representative
7. Campaign ⟶ project to achieve an aim
8. Redeem ⟶ exchange for goods
9. Mission ⟶ task or assignment
10. Explicit ⟶ very clear
11. consequences
12. Sociologists
13. evaluation
14. fulfil
15. generously
16. circulation
17. achievement
18. dependent
19. authorisation
20. technological
21. Manner ⟶ casually
22. Place ⟶ here
23. Time ⟶ recently
24. Frequency ⟶ often
25. Degree ⟶ too
26. Interrogation ⟶ why
27. Attitude ⟶ cool
28. Viewpoint ⟶ personally
29. Linking ⟶ however
30. Addition or deduction ⟶ only
31. end
32. end
33. end
34. middle
35. middle
36. beginning
37. beginning
38. beginning
39. beginning
40. middle
41. controversial
42. stealth
43. 'In some cases children <u>as young as seven</u> have been offered the chance to become "mini-marketeers"'.
44. '… to <u>plug</u> brands by <u>casually</u> dropping them into postings and conversations on social networking sites.'
45. 'They can earn the equivalent of £25 a week for their online <u>banter</u> — sometimes <u>promoting</u> <u>things that they may not even like</u>.'
46. 'Among the products being <u>pushed</u> are soft drinks, including Sprite and Dr Pepper, Cheesestrings and a Barbie-themed MP3 player.'
47. 'Multinational companies are using specialist marketing firms to recruit the children after they were <u>banned from setting up fake websites and blogs</u> to target young customers directly.'
48. The first quotation opposes the idea of employing children to promote products.
49. Molly did not want to give her full name because she thought she might get into trouble with the marketing company.
50. We know it is accurate because of the comment "Dubit has used so-called "brand ambassadors", ranging from seven to university age,"
51. No, the spokesman for Coca-Cola says that "brand ambassadors recruited through Dubit were over 16"
52. Robin Hilton, Dubit's marketing director, said of his recruits: "They must make people aware they are involved in a project if talking about a product or brand.
53. "hosting parties where product samples are distributed."

54. "Write down the key points in your own words and make sure it doesn't sound too rehearsed."
55. "Don't start a chat about the project — it's best to look for natural opportunities to drop it into the conversation."
56. "The agency encourages the youngsters to produce YouTube videos to help promote artists to their friends."
57. "I'll promote them even though I'm not a massive fan."
58. "They can earn the equivalent of £25 a week for their online banter…"
59. "They also said they would send me lots of cool samples in the post."
60. "Recruits are rewarded with vouchers that can be redeemed at most high street stores…"
61. "Members are rewarded with points for their promotional activities, which can be exchanged for music-related gifts."
62. "because I want to get the 50 points, I'll promote them"
63. "coach them to sound "natural and unrehearsed"."
64. "by posting comments on message boards"
65. "through instant messaging, such as MSN"
66. "hosting parties where product samples are distributed"
67. "thinking deeply about how you would describe it to your best friend …"
    Or any of the following:
    "write down the key points in your own words"
    "Be natural; be you"
    "it's best to look for natural opportunities to drop it into the conversation."
    "produce YouTube videos to help promote artists to their friends."
68. They are paid with points or vouchers which can be exchanged for products.
69. Children must provide evidence such as screenshots, links to online work and photographs to be paid.
70. Jemma says that because she wanted to get 50 points, she would "promote them even though I'm not a massive fan."

Paper 7

1. e-book
2. microchip
3. omnipresent
4. Neoclassical
5. telescope
6. treatable
7. careless
8. attractive
9. slowly
10. Vietnamese
11. Sadness, nothingness
12. Lacking energy
13. From the north
14. Stumbling, falling
15. Meadow, field
16. Yearns for, longs for, wishes for, grieves for
17. Unique, unusual
18. Constantly, repeatedly, incessantly, continually
19. Regret, remorse
20. Declares, announces, proclaims, reveals
21. The poet hears the woman calling
22. The poet begins to doubt that it is his wife and asks her to appear as she was when they first met.
23. The poet doubts that it is the woman's voice.
24. The poet realises that she is no longer alive and can only faintly hear her calling.
25. First person
26. This makes it more personal

27. The breeze
28. The wind
29. No
30. Woman much missed
31. You being ever dissolved to wan wistlessness
32. Much
33–44.

	Verse 1	Verse 2	Verse 3	Verse 4
Past	Y	Y	Y	N
Present	Y	Y	Y	Y
Future	N	N	N	N

45. Past
46. The past is the most frequent state because this is when the woman was alive.
47. Future
48. The speaker does not make any reference to the future because he cannot see one without the woman.
49. Alliteration
50. Pause
51. Sibilance
52. Alliteration
53. This suggests it is Autumn and that his death is near.
54. The aural image is repeated in the first and last lines of the poem because it is the most important sound to the speaker.
55. Hopeful
56. The words sound light and the vowels are feminine which makes them uplifting
57. Hopeful
58. The colour 'air-blue' is like a summer's sky.
59. Sad
60. He doubts that it is the woman's voice and the word 'listlessness' suggests a lack of energy.
61. Sad
62. The image of the 'wet mead' suggests that his environment is drab and dreary.
63. Sad
64. The image of the 'wind oozing thin' is unpleasant and the use of 'thorn' suggests pain.
65. Present
66. Past
67. Present
68. Past
69. Present
70. The title of the poem is appropriate because it is the woman calling that brings first hope and then pain for the speaker.

Paper 8

1. Parents may face these fines if they are unable to prevent their child from bullying other children.
2. The government has issued new guidelines because of the number of pupils who have been victims of cyber-bullying.
3. Supervise all e-communications in school and activities off-site
4. Revise their anti-bullying policies
5. Teach children how to behave appropriately in e-communications.
6. Teachers have a legal right to discipline pupils who take part in bullying.
7. To avoid a fine, parents could attend parenting classes.
8. The worst form of cyber-bullying is considered to be "happy-slapping".
9. One third of 92 victims said they did not report bullying incidents.
10. The most serious punishment for text harassment is six months in prison.

11. Processor
12. Interactive
13. Connection
14. Multimedia
15. Interface
16. Megabyte
17. Spreadsheet
18. Cartridge
19. Database
20. Program
21. Manners
22. Care, attention, observation
23. Required , obligatory, necessary
24. Violence, antagonism, hostility
25. Similar, like
26. <u>Persistent</u> = adjective
27. <u>Tough</u> = adjective
28. <u>Misery</u> = noun
29. <u>Firm</u> = adjective
30. <u>Worst</u> = adjective
31. If they fail to tackle their children's behaviour, parents of persistent school bullies could face fines of up to £1000.
32. E-communications on the school site or as part of school activities off-site will need to be monitored by the school under the guidelines.
33. In the compulsory anti-bullying policies, schools should account for cyber-bullying.
34. Before their parents face any fine, pupils must have been excluded once or suspended twice.
35. Bullying incidents were not reported by one third of victims.
36. The active voice makes the article more direct.
    Example Answers
37. Parents should take the responsibility of dealing effectively with any bullying behaviour their children may become involved in.
38. Parents would be extremely upset if their own child was being bullied and would want something to be done about it.
39. They have a duty to protect other people's children from such behaviour.
40. Many children have unlimited access to the internet and mobile in their bedrooms which makes monitoring e-communications at home difficult for parents.
41. It would be better if children used the internet in a communal room such as the dining room which would make them less likely to behave in a bullying way over the internet.
42. This would encourage a child to show their parents immediately if they were the victims of cyber-bullying or it could be seen from their behaviour more easily.
43. Parents need to encourage children to talk about bullying or being bullied and realise that it might take some time for their child to respond.
44. It might be helpful to raise the subject after viewing a television programme where bullying has occurred.
45. This would help the child to realise that they are not on their own.
46–48. Texting, picture messaging, emails, blogs, chatrooms, posts to social networking sites, on-line discussion forums,
49. The school has this responsibility because it has equipment that the children are using onsite or as part of their education.
    Example Answers
50. The volume of internet traffic would be difficult to monitor.
51. During break times, cyber-bullies could use their phones to text.
52. Many children have access to social networking sites on their phones.
53. The school could block social networking sites from their network.

54. The school could make it a policy that they do not allow mobile phones on site.
55. The school could make it a policy that children hand in mobiles at the start of the school day for collection at the end of the school day.
56. Schools must teach pupils e-etiquette to show them how to communicate properly in the various forms of e-communication.
    Example Answers
57. Consider the types of informal e-communications that might cause offence.
58. To adapt their style of writing to the purpose of the communication
59. To think carefully if they would be happy to receive a cyber message before they send it.
60. No, the Education and Inspections Bill would give teachers this legal right.
61. The government has given such importance to reducing instances of cyber-bullying because the majority of young people today have unlimited access to different types of e-communication.
62. The incidents of bullying will be higher than reported in the article because at least 1 in five children do not tell anyone that they have been or are being bullied.
    Example Answers
63. I do not agree that this is the worst form of cyber bullying because all types of bullying cause distress and upset for the victim concerned.
64. According to Professor Smith, psychologists have had to change their view about bullying because the methods of bullying are no longer physical and now they think that girls are more likely to take part in bullying behaviours such as rumour spreading.
65. The article ends with this sentence to remind the reader of the serious consequences of cyber bullying.
66. The headline is effective because it suggests that parents have been fined a lot of money and uses the word 'slapped' taken from the bullying form of "happy slapping".
67. The article is aimed at parents because the headline dramatically draws attention to what might happen if they could not stop their children from bullying others.
68. The sub-article has capitals to draw attention to the content.
69. The layout could be improved by using bullet points to separate each of the help lines.
70. The article suggests that parents are ultimately responsible for children who are cyber-bullies because of the headline.

Paper 9
1. Northland Wild
2. 'the savage, frozen-hearted Northland Wild.'
3. The writer only states the general area rather than setting it in a precise country.
4. Hostile, silent and menacing
5. 'There was a hint in it of laughter, but of laughter more terrible than any sadness…'
6. Suggests the landscape mocks mankind
7. Conflict between life and the wild
8. '…wisdom of eternity laughing at the futility of life and the effort of life.'
9. Contrasts eternity with the outcome of life which is death
10. The first rebellious signs of life in the landscape
11. 'But there *was* life, abroad in the land and defiant.'
12. Contrasting connective and italics highlight the contradiction of isolation in the first paragraph.
13. Two men
14. 'toiled a man' and 'toiled a second man.'
15. The repetition of 'toiled' indicates that merely walking is extreme physical labour.
16. They are carrying a coffin on their sled which connects with conflict in the first paragraph.

17. '...the Wild had conquered and beaten down until he would never move nor struggle again.'
18. Wild personified as victoriously powerful
19. A dead man
20. 'On the sled, in the box, lay a third man whose toil was over,'
21. Repetition of toil connects him to the other two men.
22. Covered by frost and snow crystals so they look like spirits
23. 'undertakers in a spectral world at the funeral of some ghost.'
24. Effective metaphor connects coffin and icy environment to the men
25. Silence oppresses them
26. 'It crushed them… pressing out of them, like juices from the grape, all the false ardours and exaltations and undue self-values of the human soul'
27. Powerful simile indicates the silence takes away all the positive things about being alive.
28. A wild, hungry cry.
29. 'It soared upward with a swift rush, till it reached its topmost note, where it persisted, palpitant and tense,'
30. Cry described as powerful and throbbing
31. The cries come from behind the men and are the first things to break the silence.
32. '…piercing the silence with needle-like shrillness.'
33. The verb 'piercing' and 'needle-like' suggests danger and possibly teeth as in the title White Fang.
34. The Wild
35. The opening suggests that they will be broken and beaten by the Wild.
36. exaltations (line 39)
37. prominent (line 17)
38. dictum (line 26)
39. infallibility (line 7)
40. traversed (line 49)
41. colossal (line 32)
42. cessation (line 26)
43. desolation (line 3)
44. palpitant (line 44)
45. mirthless (line 6)
46. toil (line 20)
47. futility (line 7)
48. indomitable (line 27)
49. spectral (line 30)
50. tangible (line 35)
51. ardour (line 38)
52. personification
53. simile
54. personification of the wild and metaphor of eternity laughing at the efforts of life.
55. simile
56. repeated imagery of the coffin
57. personification
58. listing of three
59. metaphor
60. personification
61. metaphor
62. simile
63. simile
64. personification
65. It is effective because it makes the Wild into a character to battle with humanity.
66. This is to give increased importance to setting the scene of the Wild.
67. It suggests that the dogs are more important than the men.
68. The men are not the most important characters in the story.
69. The end of the extract suggests that the men are the meat being hunted.
70. It creates tension and makes you want to know if the men are going to escape or not.

Paper 10
1. heave (line 53)
2. felicitate (line 36)
3. champains (line 24)
4. profess (line 33)
5. opulent (line 48)
6. haply (line 63)
7. divest (line 8)
8. radiance (line 73)
9. unburdened (line 6)
10. orbs (line 75)
11. conferred (line 44)
12. liberty (line 15)
13. bond (line 55)
14. meads (line 25)
15. bounty (line 11)
16. disclaim (line 15)
17. hereditary (line 41)
18. hecate (line 74)
19. interess'd (line 47)
20. weild (line 14)
21. King Lear wants to divide his kingdom into three.
22. The purpose is "darker" because it has been kept secret.
23. Remove all of the worries of looking after the kingdom.
24. He does not want to be involved in the business of looking after the kingdom.
25. Meet his death without being weighed down by any problems.
26. He asks the question which of his daughters loves him the most.
27. 10 times (lines 10, 13, 28, 28, 47–48, 48, 52, 57, 68, 70)
28. He will give up his authority to rule.
29. He will give up his claim to own the kingdom.
30. He will give up being interested in how the kingdom is run.
31. The kingdom will be divided on the basis of which daughter loves King Lear the most.
32. Three
33. Cordelia, Regan and Goneril
34. 'Nothing, my lord.' (line 49)
35. Albany is Goneril's husband.
36. Cornwall is Regan's husband.
37. The two men from France and Burgundy.
38. She says that her husband will take half of her love, care and duty.
39. He gives her four chances to change her answer (lines 52, 57, 68, 70).
40. The pauses increase the dramatic tension.
41. She begins her speech with 'Sir' because Lear's most important status is being a King rather than a father.
42. He gives her so many pauses to show that she is thinking carefully about her answer.
43. 'our joy', 'young love', 'a third more opulent than your sisters'
44. The line means that she loves her father so much that she cannot breath or speak.
45. Shakespeare introduces the audience to Cordelia through an aside, a line that only the audience can hear.
46. Cordelia's asides tell us that she is worried about the situation and thinks carefully about her answer but hopes that her love is worth more to her father than her words.
47. King Lear asks Cordelia the question last because he is saving the best part of the kingdom for her.
48. Regan means that her sister has been too mean with her words and not announced her love strongly enough.
49. King Lear suggests that Cordelia's third would be better than her two sisters.
50. *Suggested responses:* King Lear would feel shock/ anger / surprise / think that Cordelia is joking.
51. Cordelia asks why her sisters have husbands if they say that they love their father the most.
52. King Lear rejects his daughter and disowns her.

53. *Suggested response:* As a director, I would ask the actor to gesture for a map and then open it out.
54. *Suggested response:* As a director, I would ask the actor to put his hand to his heart / turn his back on Cordelia
55. Metaphor – means that Cordelia's love for her father is much stronger than words could say.
56. Listing of three - emphasises Cordelia's love for her father.
57. Metaphor - means that she cannot put into words what she feels in her heart.
58. Listing of three - reinforces Cordelia's recognition of what her father has done for her.
59. Metaphor - shows that if Cordelia marries, she must give away her love, concern and duty to her husband.
60. Listing of three - continues to reinforce the three qualities of love, care and duty that Cordelia has for her father.
61. *Example Answer:* I do not think that dividing the Kingdom on the basis of who loves someone the most is a good decision because a King has a duty to his people and this basis suggests the King is more interested in flattery than his duty.
62. *Example Answer:* I do not believe Goneril because although she says her love makes her unable to speak; she has a lot to say about how much she claims to love King Lear.
63. Regan does not get a better share of the kingdom than her sister because King Lear says that it is 'No less in space, validity, and pleasure, /Than that conferr'd on Goneril.'

64. Cordelia's second aside tells the audience that she is honest and truthful.
65. Cordelia answers with 'Nothing' because she knows that words are not powerful enough to express how much she loves her father and that she cannot gain a 'third more opulent' than her sisters.
66. King Lear's responses to Cordelia show us that he loves her the most but is foolish because he cannot understand that her answer proves this.
67. Cordelia describes her feelings towards her father as those that a daughter should have.
68. Cordelia's responses compare favourably with her sisters who both flatter King Lear excessively which makes us think that they are only telling him what he wants to hear to get the best share of the kingdom.
69. Cordelia says that she will never marry because she loves her father too much.
70. Shakespeare encourages the audience to sympathise with Cordelia because she is put in a difficult position and shares her concerns directly with the audience through the use of asides.

Acknowledgements

p4. extract from Of Mice and Men by John Steinbeck (Penguin, 2000). Copyright © John Steinbeck, 1937, 1965. Reproduced by permission of Penguin Books Ltd

p12. text reproduced by kind permission of The Times (nisyndication.com)

p39. text reproduced by kind permission of The Times (nisyndication.com)

p51. text reproduced by kind permission of The Times (nisyndication.com)